International Wealth Success was founded by Tyler G. Hicks in 1966 to empower and educate people everywhere on successful wealth building. Every book, kit, guide, and directory is guaranteed to offer proven strategies and actionable insights to help you achieve your financial, business, and personal goals. Turn the page and move forward boldly—right here, right now...

The road to financial freedom begins with education and the courage to take action.

~ Tyler G. Hicks

The IW$ Guide to

Ultimate Credit

THE SMART ENTREPRENEUR'S STRATEGY TO REPAIR, BUILD, AND MASTER CREDIT FOR BUSINESS AND FINANCIAL SUCCESS

Tyler G. Hicks

and

International Wealth Success (IW$)

IW$ PRESS

Wilkes-Barre, PA

IW$
PRESS

ISBN-13 978-1-964205-08-3

10 9 8 7 6 5 4 3 2 1

IW$ Press is an imprint of Kallisti Publishing Inc., whose titles may be bulk purchased for business or promotional use or for special sales. Please see *https://IWSPress.com* for more information.

For any lexicographers or philologists into whose hands this book may fall, the publisher may or may not have incorporated into the text, as a stimulus and a challenge to your perspicacity, one or more deliberate errors. If you'd like to alert us to your discovery, please visit https://*readKP.com/typo*.

DESIGNED IN THE UNITED STATES

BIG DEAL FOR A CLIENT

"By the way, ***using your techniques****, we did assist our client in overcoming the largest hurdle for his deal—the $10-million firm commitment from the lender in the first position mortgage."*

A NEW CAREER

"I retired from the NFL nine years ago and ***your book on real estate has kept the big money coming in!****"*

VENTURE CAPITAL SUCCESS

"I negotiated a $100,000 venture capital loan through the ad I ran in ***the IWS Newsletter ATTAIN****. Thank you!"*

INCREASES HIS NET WORTH

*"****Your books and IWS Newsletter have helped me*** *increase my net worth from $50,000 to $471,000 in 4.5 years."*

REACHING GOALS AND SETTING NEW ONES

*"****I started reading your books*** *two years ago and have now created a partnership with two of my friends. To date we have 41 total units and we're looking for more."*

FINANCIAL INDEPENDENCE

*"****Using the books and your newsletter****, I went from being on Social Security Disability to good health and a net worth of over $200,000 in the past few years. Your material works! And I'm still making progress towards my goals!"*

CAREER SWITCH SUCCESS

"I left a good-paying job two years ago to go into the carpet business. This business has become ***very successful after following the principles in the book.****"*

BUSINESS PLAN WORKS

*"****After receiving your great guide*** *on preparing a winning Business Plan, I have been offered $300,000 to start my innovative bus transportation system."*

THANKS FOR THE MOTIVATION

*"****I enjoyed your books over the years*** *and finally got the nerve to buy a small investment property, and then another, and then another. It's amazing what you can do one small step at a time."*

PRAISE FOR TYLER G. HICKS AND INTERNATIONAL WEALTH SUCCESS (IW$)

ATTAINING A GOAL

*"**Using info from your publications** I recently obtained a loan to start a toy distributor business with little difficulty. I am achieving a goal."*

HIS FIRST $1,000,000

*"**Using your ideas and methods**, and especially your down-to-earth advice and guidance on real estate negotiations, I have been able to acquire 2 properties and I am well on my way to my first $1-million through two sources—real estate and an Internet advertising company."*

MAKING GOOD MONEY IN PART TIME

*"As of today, I am pulling a minimum of $19,000 per month in fees, and **increasing my earnings every month**. I expect to go full-time in this business next month as a Professional Financial Broker."*

VALUABLE CONTACTS

*"Through the **IWS Newsletter ATTAIN** I formed my own corporation and made a number of valuable international contacts that have been most profitable. **I quit my job to devote full time to my business ventures.**"*

A MODEST STARTUP

*"**I am pleased with the materials I have obtained from you.** I have taken many of your ideas and modified them to start my business. Starting with a budget of $250 I have already grossed $6,000 (in 2 weeks) and netted $2,100."*

LAUNCHES NEW CAREER

*"**Your newsletter, books and courses have been invaluable** in launching my new career at age 54. After 3 months, with 1.5 months studying your information, I have worldwide contacts. I'm handling several large loans and have earned about $21,000 in commissions. I'm organizing a nationwide meeting pertaining to my business. IWS publications are the most profitable I've ever purchased."*

CONTENTS

INTRODUCTION

WHO SHOULD READ THE IW$ GUIDE TO ULTIMATE CREDIT?

The IW$ Guide to Ultimate Credit: The Smart Entrepreneur's Strategy to Repair, Build, and Master Credit for Business and Financial Success is for the large number of consumers and small business owners who don't have the rating they feel they deserve or need. The book is also for people who have never examined their credit history or who simply need to understand how credit reporting and repair work.

Even if you have excellent credit, your credit history is so important that it's in your best interest to check your credit report regularly and remove any errors or other damaging information that you find. We'll see how to do this shortly.

A QUICK AND EASY TEST

If you answer YES to any of these questions, then you need this book . . .

1. Do you want to apply for a loan of any kind?
2. Do you make some of your purchases by credit card?
3. Have you ever been turned down for a loan, credit card, or extended payment plan?
4. Do you need credit to help you run your business or other venture?
5. Are you curious about your credit history and credit score?
6. Do you want to know how your credit status compares to the status of other people your age, income level, location, etc?

7. Would you like to maintain and protect your credit, while improving your ability to borrow?

PURPOSE OF THIS BOOK

The purpose of this book is to give you the information you need to achieve and maintain a healthy or excellent credit status. We can divide the goal of a healthy credit status into several common goals:

- ❒ **Understand your credit score**
- ❒ **Maintain and strengthen your existing credit rating**
- ❒ **Repair a bad or damaged credit history**
- ❒ **Protect your credit and personal information from misuse**
- ❒ **Obtain additional credit as needed**
- ❒ **Avoid spending a bundle of cash to improve your credit**
- ❒ **Save money every day throughout the year**

As you take steps to improve your credit, make sure to come back to these pages and review the progress you've made in meeting the goals mentioned previously and the tools shown below.

Your credit is one of the most powerful money tools you have. Yet few of us have ever been taught how to use credit wisely. Schools don't teach it. The people we owe money to—banks, credit card companies, and others—don't teach it. And our families, well, let's just say that people who learn all about credit from their families are rare.

Many of us learn the hard way—through the school of hard knocks. Many others wind up among the millions of Americans stuck with overwhelming debt, a problem credit history and an inability to obtain additional credit when needed. People with troubled credit may feel like their lives are at the mercy of the giant credit industry. They may find it difficult or impossible to get a loan, rent a car, or even send flowers. If you feel trapped, rest assured—you are not alone. There is a way out.

The aim of this book is to give you the information, tips and techniques you need to manage your credit successfully. We'll show you how you can build a lifetime of excellent credit and enjoy life at the same time.

TOOLS TO HELP YOU REACH YOUR CREDIT GOALS

Following simple steps, you can reach each of these goals and create a lifetime of excellent credit for yourself. Here are some key steps this book covers:

- ❒ **Get to Know Consumer Credit Definitions**
- ❒ **Understand Credit and Interest**
- ❒ **Know Secured and Unsecured Debt**
- ❒ **Decide on Whether You Should Get a Cash Loan**
- ❒ **Establish, Use and Protect Your Credit**

As in any self-help, business, real estate, investment or other worthwhile venture, each individual's success depends on a variety of factors. You might already have reached some of the credit goals on your own. Others you can learn from a variety of sources, including this book. Here are some key factors that can influence your credit success. Pay attention to these and you will increase your chances of credit success and mastery!

- ❒ **Your current skills and knowledge about consumer credit**
- ❒ **Understanding basic principles needed to succeed**
- ❒ **Setting short- and long-term goals to keep you moving, step by step toward your credit goals**

- ❐ **Ongoing commitment to learning as much as possible about your credit and how you can improve it**
- ❐ **Taking initiative and action to move ahead with the opportunity**

No book alone can magically eliminate all your debts, but *The IW$ Guide to Ultimate Credit* can give you the tools you need to improve your credit and your life starting right now.

If you take the steps outlined in this book and you work toward the goals above, you should be on your way to better credit and fewer credit worries in a very short time. As you meet each of the goals we outine, you should feel less stressed about money and you should see your financial outlook getting brighter.

THE IW$ GUIDE TO ULTIMATE CREDIT

All you need is one salable activity to pursue in your spare time and you can become comfortably rich.

~ Tyler G. Hicks

THE IW$ GUIDE TO ULTIMATE CREDIT

All you need is one salable activity to pursue in your spare time and you can become comfortably rich.

~ Tyler G. Hicks

1

UNDERSTANDING CREDIT

To establish, use, maintain, or improve credit, it's important to understand a few basic words and ideas about credit. Most people understand their credit status better when they know these basic concepts. The paragraphs below describe the different kinds of consumer credit and terms you'll hear when working with credit.

GETTING STARTED

In everyday speech, people use the term "credit" in a personal sense, as in "He has good credit," "I need to build up my credit," and "I'm applying for credit with a department store." In this sense, "credit" usually means credit history, credit status, credit rating or credit account. Such informal uses of "credit" are the most common. This is how credit is used in this book, unless otherwise noted.

> *A simple definition of* **credit** *is where a borrower gets something of value (a loan) from a lender and agrees to repay the amount over time.* ***Usually the borrower is required to pay interest in exchange for the loan.***

A **credit history** is a record of an individual's or company's past borrowing and repayment behavior.

CREDIT RISK AND FICO SCORES

A **credit score** or **credit rating** is a way of measuring the credit risk of a person, a corporation, or even a country. Your credit risk is reflected partly in your credit report, which is used by the three big credit reporting agencies—

- Experian

- Equifax
- TransUnion

—to calculate your credit score. Credit scores typically range from 300 (poor credit, high risk) to 850 (exceptionally good credit, low risk), depending on the scoring model. While some industry-specific scores extend higher, most consumer credit scores, including FICO and VantageScore, cap at 850.

A credit score is commonly known as a **FICO score** because it was originally created by a company named Fair Isaac Corporation (FICO), previously known as Fair, Isaac and Company. FICO scores remain the most widely used credit scores by lenders and financial institutions.

A credit score can be hurt by things like late payments, absence of credit references, and unfavorable or irresponsible credit card use. Lenders typically use a credit score to determine whether to make a loan and what interest rate to charge. Usually, the higher the credit risk, the higher the interest rate will be for a loan or line of credit. Similarly, lenders may be less likely to make a loan to the loan applicant who is a poor credit risk.

WHAT IS CONSUMER CREDIT?

A loan, credit card transaction, or purchase of goods or services where the price is not paid in full at the time of sale are common forms of credit arrangements. "Buy now—pay later" plans are also a form of consumer credit and are available to a wide range of buyers. In this book we usually talk about credit card debt because it's the most popular form of credit for most consumers and businesses. However, references to credit cards can be replaced by most other kinds of credit wherever the words appear.

HOW DOES INTEREST WORK?

Interest is the amount it costs you to borrow money or purchase goods or services for which you will pay later. If you buy an item for $100 and you end up repaying $110, the extra $10 is interest. Generally speaking, the lower the interest rate, the lower the interest charges. By law, lenders must tell you what the interest charges will be under the credit arrangement.

ARE THERE ANY OTHER COSTS OF USING CREDIT?

It is also a good idea to find out at the start of any credit arrangement if any other fees will be added to the total purchase price. Other credit costs could include registration fees, insurance, and legal fees. This information must also be disclosed by lenders. The "true" cost of a purchase will be the price of the item or service plus the amount you repay in interest charges and other credit costs.

WHAT IS A FIXED OR VARIABLE INTEREST RATE?

A **fixed interest rate** means it will remain the same for the full time it takes to repay the loan. A **variable interest rate** is one that may change over the term of the loan. For example, a credit card might start at 19.99% APR, but after the introductory period, it could rise to 24.99% based on the prime rate plus a margin. Many lenders today use rates tied to financial benchmarks like the prime rate, SOFR, or other economic indicators. This means rates fluctuate based on broader economic conditions.

WHAT ARE SECURED DEBTS?

Collateral is whatever you give to guarantee a loan. People use items such as cars, stocks, bonds, and real estate as collateral. **Secured debts** are debts guaranteed by collateral. They give creditors added protection to guarantee repayment of a loan. With secured debts, if a debtor fails to pay back a loan, the creditor has the right to seize and sell the goods used as collateral without taking court action.

HOW ARE DEBTS SECURED?

Conditional sales contracts and chattel mortgages are common methods of securing debts. A conditional sales contract is set up as a sales contract between a purchaser and a vendor, for example, a car dealership. It is "conditional" because it allows you to have and use the goods on condition that you make regular payments on the purchase price. The creditor remains the owner of the goods until the entire debt is repaid.

While conditional sales contracts and chattel mortgages still exist, many modern financing options now include installment credit agreements or lease-to-own structures. These newer options often provide more flexibility for borrowers while still securing the lender's interest in the property.

In conditional sales contracts the store may sell the contract you have signed to a lender such as a finance company. In this situation you would make regular payments to the finance company. If the goods were defective or other problems arose, the store would still have to uphold its end of the contract.

A **chattel mortgage** is a contract signed by the debtor. In the contract the debtor agrees that on failure to pay the amount owing, some of the debtor's personal property (chattel) will become property of the creditor. Chattels are items such as cars, stocks, bonds, and other personal possessions.

WHAT ARE UNSECURED DEBTS?

Unlike conditional sales contracts and chattel mortgages, an **unsecured debt** gives the creditor no additional protection to guarantee that the debtor will repay the money. The creditor relies on the debtor's good faith and promise to pay. An example of an unsecured debt is the debt that comes from using credit cards.

TYPES OF CONSUMER CREDIT

Three basic types of consumer credit are Credit Sales, Credit Cards, and Cash Loans.

Credit Sales are usually made through a retailer. If you buy an item at a retail store you may have to sign a Conditional Sales Contract or a Promissory Note detailing the repayment schedule.

Credit Cards are available from a variety of sources. Banks, trust companies and credit unions, financial institutions, finance companies and department stores ("store cards") are just some of the institutions which offer consumer credit.

Cash Loans are usually made through banks, trust companies, credit unions, and finance companies which lend money at a fixed or variable rate. The money is repaid over a set period. Large cash loans usually require collateral.

WHAT KINDS OF CASH LOANS CAN I GET?

There are four basic types of cash loans They are:

Installment Loans: These are loans for which a borrower makes regular payments, usually monthly. For example, you may take out a $3000 loan and agree to make regular monthly payments of $250 until the $3000 and the interest are paid.

Demand Loans: If you are a low-risk customer, that is, if you will have little trouble repaying the loan or if you have the assets to cover the loan, you may get a demand loan. The interest rate with demand loans is usually variable. You repay over time as with installment loans. Loan payments can vary from month to month but require a minimum payment. With demand loans, the lender may demand repayment at any time.

Lines of Credit: These are set up at banks, trust companies or credit unions for customers with enough income, assets and an active checking account. There is a limit on the total amount available for you to borrow. To get this credit you pay interest charges on the amount owed and a service fee.

Home Mortgage Loans: These are common types of loans for people buying a home. This is usually a long-term arrangement.

Newer financing options have also emerged, including:

Peer-to-Peer (P2P) Loans: Online lending platforms that connect borrowers with individual investors.

Buy Now, Pay Later (BNPL) Loans: Short-term installment plans for purchases, widely used in online shopping.

Microloans: Small loans often used for business start-ups, typically under $50,000.*

2

CONSUMER CREDIT AND YOU

The goal of this section is to answer the most common questions about consumer credit. For more specfic answers to these and related questions, see your legal or accounting professional. This material does not contain a complete statement of the law on this subject. Changes in the law may occur from time to time.

WHAT ARE SOME OF THE BENEFITS OF CONSUMER CREDIT?

Credit may help you to take advantage of sales and bargain opportunities. It also gives you the immediate benefit of goods and services when you are short on cash. If you are not careful, however, credit can place you in trouble later when payments are due.

HOW HARD IS IT TO GET CREDIT?

If a borrower has collateral, capacity, character, and a good credit rating, then credit is usually available. Collateral is whatever you give to guarantee repayment of a loan. It backs up your word. It gives creditors rights to the items given if you do not make the payments as agreed. People use items such as cars, stocks, bonds, and real estate as collateral. Capacity means enough income to handle existing debt. Character refers to your dependability. How long have you worked at your present job? How have you handled previous debts? These are some of the things considered. A good credit rating means that you have a history of making all your payments on debts in full and on time. A lender will usually check your credit rating with a credit bureau (Experian, Equifax, or TransUnion). Many lenders also use proprietary scoring models, alternative credit data, and AI-driven risk assessments in addition to traditional credit reports.

CAN I REALLY IMPROVE MY CREDIT RATING?

There are several things that you can do to improve your credit rating—and they are not hard to do. For example, making payments in full and on time improves your credit rating. Getting a credit card, having your own bank account, managing household expenses, or opening a line of credit are all ways of establishing and improving your credit. Lenders use records of these transactions as indicators of your reliability as a debtor.

WHAT ARE SOME OF THE ADVANTAGES OF CREDIT CARDS?

Credit cards give you another way to buy and pay for goods and services. Generally, if your account is paid in full within a certain time, no interest charges will be added.

WHAT ARE SOME OF THE DISADVANTAGES OF USING CREDIT CARDS?

The interest rates on credit cards are usually high and vary from card to card. Shop around for the card that best suits you.

Different cards have different ways of determining interest charges. Generally speaking, bank cards calculate interest from the date the items/goods were bought.

If you use your credit card for a cash advance, interest is charged from when the money is taken. Check into these charges when applying for a credit card.

A creditor may freeze a credit card when you do not make a payment when due, if you go over your credit limit, or if you make a payment less than the minimum.

Many modern credit cards now offer tools like purchase tracking, fraud alerts, and financial management features through mobile banking apps, making it easier to stay on top of payments and spending.

Web sites and credit companies like those in the box below make it easy to browse and compare several credit card offers to get the best value for what you need.

I RECEIVED A CREDIT CARD IN THE MAIL THAT I DID NOT ASK FOR

In some locales, it is illegal for a lender to send a credit card in the mail that you did not ask for. Under the **CARD Act**, credit card issuers in the U.S. cannot send unsolicited credit cards, though pre-approved offers may still be sent via mail. If you do receive a credit card in the mail, do not use it unless you're absolutely certain you want to start an account with the lender that sent the card. If you think you should not have received the card, you can report it to your state or regional consumer affairs office or the Federal Trade Commission.

> ***Remember, use of the card, even once, is seen as acceptance of the card.***

DOES MARITAL STATUS AFFECT CREDIT?

Your ability to get credit may depend upon a credit assessment and your credit rating. If you are married the Credit Bureau usually holds a credit rating for each spouse. However, if only one spouse signs a credit agreement, generally the other spouse's credit rating is not checked. When you and your spouse jointly apply for credit you may have more assets. If you and your spouse both have income, you will have a greater capacity to repay any loans. This will improve your chances of getting credit. Separation or divorce does not automatically deny you access to credit. Lenders place much emphasis on your credit rating. If you do not have a separate credit rating, it may take you time to set one up. Lenders will usually look at your income, what you own and what you owe before deciding.

WHO IS RESPONSIBLE FOR JOINT CREDIT CARD DEBTS?

Credit card debt is always the responsibility of the person who signed the card. If you apply for a card and ask for a second one for your spouse, both of you will be responsible for any debt placed on that card. This remains the same despite changes in marital status. However, if one spouse is an authorized user rather than a joint account holder, they are not legally responsible for the debt.

HOW CAN I END MY RESPONSIBILITY ON A JOINT CREDIT CARD?

Upon separation or divorce there are several ways to end your responsibility on a joint credit card. If it is not possible to get the card back you can visit your lender to change your account and thus cancel your responsibility for future debts. You may also see your lender to sign a Statement of Non-Responsibility. This signed statement will end your responsibility for future debts.

AM I RESPONSIBLE FOR MY SPOUSE'S PERSONAL BANK LOANS?

If you sign or cosign a loan, then you are liable for repayment of the debt unless the lender agrees in writing to cancel your responsibility. As with credit cards your responsibility for credit contracts, such as bank loans remains the same despite changes in marital status. Upon separation or divorce a Court may decide one spouse is responsible for the debts. If that spouse decides not to continue making payments then he/she can be found in contempt of a court order.

GET HOME AND BUSINESS LOANS DESPITE POOR CREDIT

Do you need a home mortgage loan? Or a loan for your future, or existing business? If you do, there's good news, even if you have poor credit. Here it is:

Lenders rate borrowers by levels of credit—A, B, C, or D. Here's how they do this.

A credit = A person with **excellent credit** (740+ FICO score), no history of late pays, slow pays, or no pays.

B credit = People with **good credit** (670–739 FICO score), a few missed or late payments, but the payments were eventually made.

C credit = People with **fair credit** (580–669 FICO score), some late payments, higher credit utilization, or past credit issues.

D credit = A **subprime borrower** (below 580 FICO), late payments, defaults, collections, or bankruptcy.

> ***Any loan to a borrower with less than A credit is called a subprime loan and a higher interest rate is charged to the borrower, compared to rates charged to individuals with A, B or C credit rating.***

Today lenders are finding that:

- **Subprime borrowers can get loans after the lender carefully considers their credit history, employment stability, and ability to pay.**
- **Subprime lending is a multi-billion-dollar market.** Lenders may offer more or fewer subprime loans depending on economic conditions.
- **Subprime borrowers can improve their credit rating by repaying new loans on time and managing debt wisely.**
- **Subprime borrowers mostly seek loans for home mortgages—either a new first mortgage to reduce**

payments and perhaps get some cash out of the transaction or a home equity loan for cash.

If you, or one of your clients, is a subprime borrower, you may be able to get the loan you need by taking these easy steps:

- **Find out why you or the person or business seeking the loan has a subprime credit rating.** Get a copy of your credit report and list all slow pays, double pays, and other less-than-perfect repayment records. Any time you're turned down for a loan, you can get a copy of your credit report for free.
- **List the causes of slow pays, double pays, and any other nonperformance by the borrower.** If there are any errors in the report, contact the credit company and lodge a written dispute about the errors.
- **Prepare a detail sheet showing each slow pay or late pay and give the reason alongside each date.** Show when the payment was made, and how the borrower caught up with the payment schedule.
- **Give detail sheet to the lender when you apply.** With a bit of luck you'll get the loan!
- **Subprime lenders sometimes help prospective borrowers get a loan by recommending a credit counselor, The counselor gets the borrower's credit straightened out so the person is eligible for the needed loan.**

HEADING OFF FINANCIAL DISASTER

A large part of improving credit depends on knowing the warning signs that mean you're living beyond your means. You need to get a grip on your finances as quickly as possible if:

❐ **You spend more than 15%–25% of your take-**

home pay on credit card or loan payments (not including a mortgage).

- ❒ You rely on "Buy Now, Pay Later" loans or payday loans to cover basic necessities.
- ❒ You have no idea how much debt you owe.
- ❒ You can't make minimum payments on your credit cards.
- ❒ You don't have an emergency fund for unexpected expenses.

WHAT CAN I DO TO AVOID (OR GET OUT OF) FINANCIAL TROUBLE?

- ❒ **Stop borrowing immediately.**
- ❒ **Take a close look at your lifestyle to see where the money problems arose.**
- ❒ **Contact your creditors (people to whom you owe money).** Creditors do not like to push anyone into default (inability to meet their financial obligations).
- ❒ **Contact your creditors and ask whether you can work (that is, negotiate) a deal that will reduce what you owe or give you additional time to pay.**
- ❒ **If financial counseling is available through a community agency get advice on dealing with your money problems.**
- ❒ **Many people in this situation have found it helpful to use an inexpensive legal service such as Prepaid Legal, Inc.** or an attorney to get the amount reduced. Don't underestimate their power to help you.
- ❒ **Establish a well-planned budget.**
- ❒ **Set realistic goals for yourself so you can see each step of progress you make.** You can turn your credit

woes into a healthy credit portfolio. Millions of people have done it.

3

HOW TO ESTABLISH, USE, AND PROTECT YOUR CREDIT

WHAT YOU NEED TO KNOW

Good credit is valuable. Having the ability to borrow funds allows us to buy things we would otherwise have to save for years to afford: homes, cars, a college education. Credit is an important financial tool, but it can also be dangerous, leading people into debt far beyond their ability to repay. That is why learning how to use credit wisely is one of the most valuable financial skills anyone can learn.

This section covers:

- ❒ **What Lenders Look For**
- ❒ **How to Establish Credit**
- ❒ **Protecting Credit**
- ❒ **Common Reasons for Denying Credit**
- ❒ **Improving Poor Credit**
- ❒ **Divorce and Credit**
- ❒ **Paying Off a Loan Early**
- ❒ **For More Information**

WHAT LENDERS LOOK FOR

Before creditors lend money, they need to be assured that the funds will be repaid. In other words, is the prospective borrower creditworthy? To find out, they ask for various

Income & Expenses

Lenders will look at what you earn and your regular expenses, such as rent, utilities, food, and other ongoing items. The amount left tells them whether you can afford to take on additional debt.

Assets

Do you have assets that can serve as collateral? Lenders will look for things like bank accounts, insurance, and valuable items such as a house, if you own one.

Credit History

How do you manage debt? If you have credit cards or have borrowed money before, you have a history that shows prospective lenders whether you are creditworthy by revealing details about the amount of debt you already have, how many credit cards you have, and whether you make payments on time.

It's easy to qualify for credit if you have a good credit history, but what if you have never used credit before? This is a common problem for people who just started working, those who work in the home, people who always pay in cash, and those who do not have assets or accounts in their own names. For them, the first step is to establish a credit history.

POTENTIAL WAYS OF ESTABLISHING CREDIT

Begin by opening individual savings and checking accounts in your name. Over time, your deposits, withdrawals, and transfers will demonstrate that you can handle money responsibly.

Applying for a loan is another option, but be aware that this method of establishing a credit history will cost, since loans require the payment of interest.

You could take out a bank loan secured by the funds you have on deposit or by items you own, such as a car. You could also ask a friend or relative who has good credit to cosign a loan, which means that he or she shares liability for the loan with you.

You could also apply for department store and gasoline credit cards, which generally are easier to obtain than major credit cards. Before you apply for any credit, however, make sure you understand the terms.

For example, how long is the grace period or the time you have to pay the current balance in full before finance charges are added? Is there an annual fee or other fees associated with the credit?

If you believe that you will carry a balance, you need to know how finance charges are calculated. Patience is important in this process. It takes time to establish credit and build a record of consistency in making payments to demonstrate your creditworthiness. And it is much better to go slowly and develop a strong credit record than to apply for too many credit cards or a loan that is larger than you can handle.

Start slowly, be cautious, keep track of your overall debt, and pay on time. Most importantly, remember that credit actually represents real money and has to be repaid with interest.

PROTECTING YOUR CREDIT

Once you have obtained credit, it is necessary to protect it. This means being careful with your credit, debit, and ATM cards, as well as your account and personal identification numbers (PIN). Carry only the cards you expect to use, and keep the others in a safe place. Maintain a list of account and telephone numbers of the companies that issued your cards. Then, if the cards are lost or stolen, you can notify the companies quickly.

If your notification is received before the cards are used, you have no legal responsibility for the bills; if it is received after the cards are used, your legal responsibility is $50 for each card.

Be cautious about giving anyone your account numbers, especially over the telephone when someone calls you. Save sales receipts to compare with your bill, and when you discard documents with account numbers on them, be sure the numbers can't be read.

If you disagree with an item on a bill, you are responsible for notifying the creditor in writing within 60 days of receiving the bill. You should include your name, account number, the item you believe is in error, and the reasons why.

Freezing Your Credit for Added Protection

A credit freeze prevents lenders from pulling your credit report, stopping fraudsters from opening accounts in your name. You can request a freeze for free at the websites of Experian, Equifax, and TransUnion. You can also temporarily lift a freeze when applying for credit.

Fraud Alerts and Identity Theft Protections

If you suspect fraud, you can place a free fraud alert on your credit report. A fraud alert notifies creditors to take extra steps to verify identity before opening new accounts.

For identity theft concerns, visit the Federal Trade Commission (FTC) website at *www.identitytheft.gov* for official recovery steps.

NATIONAL FOUNDATION FOR CREDIT COUNSELING (NFCC)

The NFCC provides credit counseling and financial education through a network of nonprofit agencies across the U.S. If you're seeking a Consumer Credit Counseling Service (CCCS) agency, make sure it's a legitimate NFCC member. Some imitators charge unnecessary fees for services that true CCCS agencies provide for free.

According to the NFCC, more than one-third of all consumers who seek help from NFCC agencies are able to manage their debt independently after receiving financial counseling.

National Foundation for Credit Counseling
2000 M St NW, Suite 505

Washington, DC 20036
Phone: 800-388-2227
Website: *www.nfcc.org*

THE "BIG THREE" CREDIT REPORTING AGENCIES

Consumers can request their free credit reports weekly from each of the three major credit bureaus at *AnnualCreditReport.com*. Below are their current contact details:

Experian
P.O. Box 4500
Allen, TX 75013
Phone: 888-EXPERIAN (888-397-3742)
Website: *www.experian.com*

Equifax
P.O. Box 740256
Atlanta, GA 30374-0256
Phone: 888-548-7878
Website: *www.equifax.com*

TransUnion
P.O. Box 2000
Chester, PA 19016
Phone: 800-916-8800
Website: *www.transunion.com*

4

IMPROVING POOR CREDIT

Common reasons people are turned down when applying for credit:

- Too little time in current job or at current residence
- Too much outstanding debt
- Unreasonable purpose for requesting credit
- Cosigner cannot take on additional debt liability
- Errors on applicant's credit report
- Unusually stringent standards by creditors

In general, creditworthiness must be determined on the basis of criteria that relate to your ability and willingness to repay debt. You cannot be denied credit based on your sex, marital status, race, religion, national origin, age, or dependence on income from public assistance. If you are denied credit, the creditor must provide you with a written statement of the action and your rights, as well as the reason for denial or how to request the reason.

YOUR ACTION STEPS

If you've fallen behind in your payments, begin immediately to repair your credit record. Following are popular action steps you can take today.

❒ *Action Step:* **Recognize that you (or someone with access to your credit cards) have created a large amount of debt for yourself.** You might have put yourself in a situation where you are1 so overextended that you can't even pay your bills. This is also known as overextending your credit. Commit yourself to learning the best ways to improve your credit and your credit history. Do it now!

- ❒ *Action Step:* **Contact your creditors to see if they will set up a new payment schedule that you can maintain.** In any case, don't ignore your bills.
- ❒ *Action Step:* **Immediately stop using your credit to buy or rent anything with credit.** Take your credit cards out of your wallet. If you must use a card, use a debit (ATM) card. Because debit cards are linked directly to your bank account, you'll probably be less inclined to charge large or expensive items.
- ❒ *Action Step:* **Try storing your credit cards in a spot that is hard to reach.** If you want, cut them up. You can probably come up with more creative ways to discourage yourself from using your credit cards.

One consumer we know actually puts her credit cards in a glass of water and then freezes the glass in the kitchen freezer. She rarely uses the card because it's such a pain to thaw it out. By the time it's thawed, she's had about 2 hours to think above what she's doing. In this period of time, she may decide not to use the card and put it back in the freezer.

- ❒ *Action Step:* **Consider consolidating your debts.** When you consolidate your debts— credit cards, car payments, insurance, utilities, even your mortgage— you roll them all into one debt and pay off the consolidated amount each month, over time. Most people find it easier to make a single monthly payment to one account than having to worry about several different accounts with separate payment dates, due dates, minimum payments, addresses and so on.

A big part of the job of any good credit counseling firm is to work with your creditors to consolidate debts, reduce interest rates, and reduce or eliminate certain debts. When you talk with your banker or a reputable consumer credit organization regarding debt consolidation, you can ask whether you might be eligible for a reduction in your interest rate on the consolidated debt.

Be persistent and let the lender know that the reduced interest will help you pay your monthly bill. Remember that debt consolidation is not a cure-all. Although it can be a great help, you still have to learn to control your spending to avoid future debt.

- ❒ *Action Step:* **Contact a credit counseling organization.** But be aware that the quality can vary a lot from firm to firm. You can obtain referrals for organizations in your area through the National Foundation for Credit Counseling (NFCC), Check them out at *www.nfcc.org/* or by phone at (800) 388-2227.

The **U.S. Trustee Program** (part of the Department of Justice) reviews and approves credit counseling agencies across the U.S. If you need credit counseling, check their official list of approved firms at:

Executive Office for U.S. Trustees
441 G Street NW, Suite 6150
Washington, DC 20530
Phone: 202-514-4100
Website: *www.justice.gov/ust*

The U.S. Trustee's website includes contact details and indicates whether a counseling agency offers services in-person, online, or by phone. Checking this list ensures that you are working with a reputable, approved agency.

The Trustee Program is the component of the Department of Justice responsible for overseeing the administration of bankruptcy cases, private trustees and credit counseling agencies. Many agencies are being added to the U.S. Trustee's office of approved credit counseling agencies each day.

The Trustee web site also includes each agencies' contact information and tells the main ways they do business—in person, over the phone, through the Internet, or a combination of these. U.S. Trustee's office might be able to help you find a reputable credit counselor who will work with you to get your finances on track.

Not all credit counseling firms are reputable. Some charge high fees for services that legitimate nonprofit organizations provide for free or at low cost. Before working with any firm, check:

- **National Foundation for Credit Counseling (NFCC):** *www.nfcc.org*
- **U.S. Trustee's List of Approved Agencies:** *www.justice.gov/ust*
- **Better Business Bureau (BBB):** *www.bbb.org*

Warning: Avoid companies that promise to "erase" bad credit for a fee. No company can legally remove accurate negative information from your credit report.

You can start building and improving your credit rating as fast as it takes to read this book. But no one—including credit counseling agencies—can erase negative information from your credit record if the information is accurate and up to date.

The Better Business Bureau Can Help

The Better Business Bureau monitors businesses throughout the U.S. and produces reports on the companies for consumers and other business people. BBB reports reveal whether anyone has reported complaints on a given company and how frequent the complaints were. The BBB is an extremely important tool to use when evaluating any credit repair agency. BBB reports should be seen as one of a number of key resources to check before using a credit agency. Others are the U.S. Trustee's Office and the National Foundation for Credit Counseling. See separate Resource Box for more information.

The Council of Better Business Bureaus
4200 Wilson Blvd, Suite 800
Arlington, VA 22203-1838
Phone: 1 (703) 276.0100
Fax: (703) 525.8277
www.bbb.org

The Canadian Council of Better Business Bureaus
2 St. Clair Ave.
East Toronto, ON M4T 2T5
Telephone: (416) 644-4936
Fax: (416) 644-4945
www.ccbb.ca

CREDIT REPORTING AGENCIES

The slow and steady course toward fixing bad credit might not be what you hoped for. Nevertheless, it's a fact that one of the best, and often the fastest, ways to improve your credit history is to get a copy of your credit report from one or more of the three major credit reporting agencies (also called credit bureaus). These three bureaus are Experian, Equifax or TransUnion—and then review and "clean up" your reports as thoroughly as possible.

Your credit report is a computerized profile of your borrowing, charging, and repayment activities. Any time you apply for credit and your application is turned down, you're entitled by law to get one copy of your credit report from one of the credit reporting agencies for free.

Federal law allows you to get a free credit report from each of the three major bureaus every 12 months at www.annualcreditreport.com. As of recent updates, you can now access free weekly reports from this site.

It's strongly recommended that you get a copy from all three of the credit reporting firms at the same time. This is because there are usually differences between each report. Because of the way they collect data,, none of the credit bureaus has exactly the same information on you at the same time. Such differences could affect your credit rating. It's best to get all three.

Your FICO score is an important part of your credit history. It ranges from 300 to 850, with higher scores showing better creditworthiness.

You may be able to get your FICO score for free from:

- **Your credit card provider (many banks offer free FICO scores)**
- **Experian, Equifax, or TransUnion (some provide scores for free)**
- **www.myfico.com (official source for purchasing FICO scores)**

Important: Some free credit scores (like those from Credit Karma) use VantageScore, which may differ from the FICO score lenders use.

One of the most important ways to fix your credit history is to find any and all incorrect or out-of-date data in your report and dispute the information with the credit reporting firm and with the individual creditor with whom you have (or had) the disputed account details.

FIND OUT IF A CREDIT-COUNSELING FIRM IS APPROVED

The U.S. Trustee Program (part of the Department of Justice) reviews and approves credit counseling agencies across the U.S. If you need credit counseling, check their official list of approved firms at:

Executive Office for U.S. Trustees
441 G Street NW, Suite 6150

Washington, DC 20530
Phone: 202-514-4100
Website: www.justice.gov/ust

The U.S. Trustee's website includes contact details and indicates whether a counseling agency offers services in-person, online, or by phone. Checking this list ensures that you are working with a reputable, approved agency.

Many agencies are added to the approved list each day. The Web site also includes the credit counseling agencies' contact information and how they do business—in person, over the phone or through the Internet. Th U.S. Trustee's office is a valuable resource. They can help you find a good counselor to help you get your credit and spending back on right track.

DIVORCE AND CREDIT

Aside from its non-financial effects, divorce can cause problems with your credit record. The end of a marriage does not erase the debts you and your former spouse took on as a couple. Even if your former spouse is ordered by the court to pay debts from the marriage, you can become liable if they are not paid. Here are a few suggestions to protect your financial standing:

- ❒ **Decide how to divide or dispose of property.** If necessary, you can use a mediator to work through this with your former spouse.
- ❒ **Close or separate joint accounts.**
- ❒ **Together with your ex-spouse or soon-to-be ex-spouse, decide which one of you will be responsible for paying particular bills.** Notify your creditors of your divorce.
- ❒ **Establish independent credit, if you do not already have it.** Make sure you look at your credit reports hard for any joint accounts, cosigner agree-

ments, loans and any other financial agreements made with your spouse. If you have joint accounts or agreements like those we just cited, your credit rating could be dragged down because your ex-spouse has a bad credit rating.

PAYING OFF A LOAN EARLY

If you are applying for a loan and think you may want to pay it off before it has run its full term, you should be aware that lenders have several methods of calculating interest. The method they use affects the amount you will owe if you decide to pay off early. Since lenders are not required to disclose which method they use, you may have to ask. Here is a brief description of the most common interest-calculation methods.

"Rule of 78"

A standard loan is called "simple interest". You borrow some money and at the end of the period you pay it back plus interest. For longer term loans, you make periodic payments. With some consumer loans, especially with auto loans, you may encounter a different type of loan which mentions the "Rule of 78". This "rule" is a different way of deciding how much of each monthly payment is interest and how much is principal.

If you don't terminate the loan early, simple interest loans and Rule of 78 loans will be roughly the same. You'll pay the same amount and get the interest rate quoted. If you pay off the loan early, however, you'll end up paying more interest with a Rule of 78 loan than with the corresponding "simple interest" loan. For that reason, many experienced borrowers and investors recommend that you should not take loans computed on the "Rule of 78".

The Rule of 78 method uses tables based on a mathematical formula to determine how much interest you have paid at any point during a loan. It requires that you pay more interest at the beginning of a loan when you have the use of more of the money and that you pay less interest as the debt is reduced.

Since all of your payments are the same in amount, the amount of your payment that is going toward the principal increases while the amount going toward interest decreases. Some locales may mandate the use of the Rule of 78.

Generally, the longer the term of a loan and the higher the interest rate, the less favorable the Rule of 78 is to borrowers who wish to pay off early. However, for loans of less than five years and with interest lower than 15 percent, the payoff calculated by the Rule of 78 is similar to that calculated with the actuarial method, described below.

Actuarial Method

This method is most often used for mortgages and other loans in which a periodic rate is applied to a declining balance. It does not take into consideration whether a payment is made before or after the due date. Late payments are subject to a flat penalty, but interest does not continue to accrue.

Daily Simple Interest

In this method, a daily periodic rate is applied to an outstanding balance. Therefore, borrowers benefit by reducing the outstanding balance through early payments or lump-sum payments, both of which reduce the balance and the interest due. Under a simple interest system, late payers will end up owing more.

PULLING CREDIT

If you're in business or seeking to make money in real estate, you've probably had to get a credit report for yourself or a client. Getting your copy of the report is called "pulling credit." It's easy to do, but expensive. Most people who pull credit want to know: "How can I pull credit without breaking the bank?" Here are some creative suggestions.

- Most of us are familiar with single or triple-bureau credit reports priced at $30 and higher; of course most people want to pay $0-$10 per report.
- One school of thought is to charge additional amounts for processing the reports. In other words, you might charge your client a report-pulling fee; then, you don't have to swallow those fees anymore.
- Before ordering multiple credit reports on your client, get one report to make sure your client has a "snowball's chance" of getting the loan.
- If you think your client may be able to get the loan, you can pull the other two bureaus' reports for additional details.
- See if the credit bureau will give you discounts for ordering multiple reports.
- Some companies like Credit Plus and Funding Suite software charge around $10 for triple-bureau reports.

45 WAYS TO BETTER CREDIT

Many people can't get the credit they need to build a business or to open a business or do a real estate deal. Armed with the right information, however, credit-seekers have a better chance of getting the money they seek. It's not always necessary to have a lengthy credit history or an 800-plus FICO score. Here are 45 no-nonsense ways that real credit experts use to clear away barriers to success. Nearly anyone can use the techniques below to turn poor credit into good (or better-than-good) credit.

1. Apply to several lenders. You only need one to say yes.
2. Earn more income to pay off existing debts faster.
3. Make all current account payments on time. In other words, don't dig deeper into the money pit.
4. Use auto-pay and reminders. Late payments can

drastically impact your score, so set up auto-pay or phone alerts.

5. Ask certain creditors—such as doctors or dentists—if they'll let payments be stretched out over time.
6. If possible, avoid getting new credit cards while working to clean up old debts.
7. Avoid illegal schemes like those using Social Security data and promising a "new identity."
8. Legitimate credit repair firms do exist, but many credit experts say they're not needed.
9. Save money. Don't pay a commercial credit repair firm to do the work. Anyone can do it.
10. Check with universities, credit unions, military bases, etc., for free and low-cost credit help.
11. Visit a free nonprofit or government-run credit-counseling service for detailed tips and advice.
12. Through free or low-cost credit counselors, find out how to order and read a credit report.
13. For safety, send letters on credit matters by certified mail, "return receipt requested."
14. Keep copies or notes on all correspondence that you have with creditors and credit bureaus.
15. Before applying for new credit with a lender or vendor, find out what credit bureau they use.
16. Call the lender or vendor to ask what guidelines they use to approve a credit application.
17. Ask the lender exactly what it will need in terms of business data and documents.
18. Using the information from the lender, send for the credit report that the creditor uses.

19. Get a copy of the credit report from the credit bureau (Experian, Equifax, TransUnion, etc.).
20. Whenever credit is denied, the credit bureau must provide a free report within 30 days upon request.
21. Check your credit report regularly. Consumers can now check their credit reports for free weekly at AnnualCreditReport.com.
22. Read the report or have someone else read it, recalling what the credit counselor has said.
23. Scan the report for any possible errors or inaccuracies and unfamiliar or unsure information.
24. Write down any and all errors or bad information found in the credit report.
25. Call or write the credit bureau for the form used to submit complaints about bad data.
26. Put all complaints and possible bad data on the form and mail it to the credit bureau.
27. By law, the original creditor must confirm old data (in about 20 days), or the bureau removes it.
28. If the bureau doesn't hear from the creditor or the creditor can't confirm the bad data, it's removed.
29. If some creditors have been paid regularly on time, send this and other good data to the bureau too.
30. Also include this good data, along with a brief explanation, in applications for new credit.
31. The credit bureau tells the debtor of changes in the report resulting from the debtor's complaints.
32. When the bureau's letter comes, make sure the creditor gets a copy of the new, improved report.

33. Show lenders that honest efforts are underway to pay existing debts.
34. Negotiate with creditors for ways to work around doubts that the credit record caused them earlier.
35. For example, creditors might agree to make a loan based on a special repayment plan.
36. If everything else has already been tried, consider selling some possessions to help pay off debts.
37. Consolidate debt with a home equity loan or other such arrangement.
38. Refinance a home mortgage to get more cash in hand.
39. Get loans from family or friends if possible.
40. Borrow against life insurance.
41. Use a secured credit card if needed. A secured card with a refundable deposit can help rebuild credit.
42. Consider credit-builder loans. Many credit unions offer small installment loans designed to improve your score.
43. Be careful with "Buy Now, Pay Later" services. These installment plans are popular but can lead to over-spending and affect credit if mismanaged.
44. Use fintech apps to track and improve your credit. Many apps now offer personalized credit insights and improvement tips.
45. Build positive credit history by using existing credit responsibly and maintaining low balances.

5

YOUR CREDIT REPORT AND WHAT IT SAYS ABOUT YOU

Most people finance their homes with mortgages and pay for their cars with loans. Young people often obtain loans to pay for college. And, of course, lots of people make purchases with credit cards.

You can't expect to receive credit as a matter of course, however. You must apply for it. And just as you would hesitate to lend money to a stranger, banks, retailers, or finance companies will not grant you credit without knowing something about you.

It used to be that a retailer or bank would have to call each creditor you listed on an application form before they would decide to extend credit to you. Today, they rely on credit reports, so it's important for you to know what is in yours.

SOURCES OF HELP FROM THE FEDERAL GOVERNMENT

You can contact the following agencies of the U.S. Government with auestions and concerns about credit agencies and their business practices. An expanded list of these and other help sources is at the back of this book.

Federal Trade Commission (FTC)
Consumer Response Center - FCRA
600 Pennsylvania Avenue, NW Washington, D.C. 20580 (877) FTC-HELP
www.ftc.gov

Federal Reserve Consumer Help
PO Box 1200
Minneapolis, MN 55480
Phone: 888-851-1920
TDD: 877-766-8533
Fax: 877-888-2520
E-mail: *ConsumerHelp@FederalReserve.gov*

Federal Deposit Insurance Corporation (FDIC)
Consumer Response Center 2345 Grand Blvd., Suite 100 Kansas City, MO 64108
Phone: 877-ASK-FDIC (275-3342)
E-mail: *consumeralerts@fdic.gov*

WHAT IS A CREDIT REPORT?

A credit report is a record of your credit activities. It lists any credit-card accounts or loans you may have, the balances, and how regularly you make your payments. It also shows if any action has been taken against you because of unpaid bills.

Where Do Credit Reports Come from?

A company that gathers and sells credit information is called a **consumer reporting agency** (CRA). These types of companies collect information about your credit activities, store it in giant databases, and charge a fee for supplying the information. The most common type of CRA is the credit bureau.

There are three major credit bureaus that operate nationwide, plus many smaller companies serving local markets.

How Can I Obtain a Copy of my Credit Report?

You are entitled to receive one free credit report every 12 months from each of the three nationwide credit bureaus—Equifax, Experian, and TransUnion. The official site for requesting your report is *AnnualCreditReport.com*, where you can order it online, by phone, or by mail.

Additionally, as of recent regulatory updates, consumers can now access free weekly credit reports through 2026 to monitor their credit more frequently. Many banks and credit card issuers also provide free access to your credit score and report within your online banking dashboard.

More Details on Credit Ratings

Your credit rating is drawn from your credit report, which outlines your borrowing, charging, and repayment activities. A good rating helps you reach financial goals; a poor rating limits your financial opportunities.

> ***Since your credit report influences whether you are able to buy a home and get a job, it is extremely important to protect your credit rating by making loan and bill payments on time and by not taking on more debt than you can handle.***

To process your request, you will need to provide specific information, such as your name, current and previous addresses, telephone number, social security number, and date of birth. Also, to verify your identity, other information such as a copy of your driver's license, utility bill(s), or bank statement may be required. These steps are meant to safeguard your identity and credit information. Keep in mind that the three large bureaus do not necessarily share information with each other. The content of your credit report can be different at each bureau, so it's a good idea to request copies from each one.

Who Is Allowed to See Your Credit Report?

Credit bureaus can only provide your report to:

1. **Lenders** evaluating your creditworthiness.
2. **Employers**, but only with your written permission before hiring or promoting you.

3. **Insurance companies** assessing policy applications or renewals.
4. **Government agencies** reviewing financial status for benefits or investigations.
5. **Landlords** verifying rental applications.

Credit bureaus also furnish reports if required by court orders or federal jury subpoenas. They will also issue your report to a third party if you request this in writing.

The Consumer Financial Protection Bureau (CFPB) has recently tightened regulations on employer credit checks, ensuring job applicants are not unfairly denied employment due to old or irrelevant credit issues.

YOUR CREDIT REPORT

What Type of Information Is On Your Credit Report?

There are usually four types of information:

1. **Identifying Information:** Your full name, any known aliases, current and previous addresses, social security number, year of birth, current and past employers, and, if applicable, similar information about your spouse.
2. **Credit Information:** The accounts you have with banks, retailers, credit-card issuers, utility companies, and other lenders (accounts are listed by type of loan, such as mortgage, student loan, revolving credit, or installment loan; the date you opened the account; your credit limit or the loan amount; any co-signers of the loan; and your payment pattern over the past two years).
3. **Public Record Information:** State and county court records on bankruptcy, tax liens, or monetary

judgments (some consumer reporting agencies list non-monetary judgments as well).

4. **Recent Inquiries:** The names of those who have obtained copies of your credit report within the past year (two years for employment purposes).

Where Do the Consumer Reporting Agencies Get Their Information?

Credit bureaus collect information from parties that have previously extended credit to you, such as a department store that issued you a credit card or a bank that granted you a personal loan.

Who Decides whether or Not to Grant You a Loan?

The lenders themselves make the decision about whether or not to grant you credit. The credit-reporting companies only supply the information about your credit history.

Why Should You Obtain a Copy of Your Credit Report?

To avoid any unwelcome surprises, it's important to see a copy of your credit report before you apply for credit such as car loans, mortgages, or credit cards. Errors in credit reports can be common. Keep in mind, however, that they are not part of a conspiracy against you. They are simply the result of human error.

How Do Errors in Reports Happen?

Think about how often your mail has a misspelling of your name or a mistake in your street address. Then, imagine the possibility for error in a report that contains much more information about you. Cases of mistaken identity, out-of-date information, and outright errors can easily occur.

How Long Does Information Stay on Your Credit Report?

The length of time varies depending on the activity:

- **Most negative marks** (late payments, charge-offs, foreclosures) remain for 7 years.
- **Bankruptcies** stay for 10 years from the filing date.
- **Hard inquiries** (when lenders check your credit for a loan application) stay for 2 years but have minimal impact after 12 months.
- **Positive accounts** (good payment history) can remain for up to 10 years after being closed.

Recent CFPB rulings have restricted **medical debt** reporting—many medical collections under $500 are now removed from reports, and paid medical debts no longer impact your score.

How Do You Correct an Error on Your Credit Report?

If you find incorrect information, dispute it immediately with both:

- **The credit bureau** (Equifax, Experian, or TransUnion).
- **The creditor** that reported the incorrect data.

The best ways to do this are:

- **Online:** All three credit bureaus now allow direct online disputes on their websites.
- **Mobile Apps:** Experian and Equifax allow disputes via mobile apps for faster processing.

If a dispute isn't resolved within 30 days, the incorrect item must be removed unless the creditor provides verifiable proof.

What if the Consumer Reporting Agency Stands by Its Report?

You have the right to present your side of the story in a brief statement (100 words or less), which the credit bureau must attach to your credit file. Your statement should be used to clarify inaccuracies, not explain reasons for delinquency.

Anyone requesting a copy of your credit report would also automatically receive your statement (or a summary of it), unless the credit bureau decides that it is irrelevant or frivolous.

What Should You Do If You Are Denied Credit Because of Something in Your Credit Report?

Under the Fair Credit Reporting Act (FCRA), if you're denied credit, the lender must provide:

- **A written notice** stating the specific reason for denial.
- **The name and contact details** of the credit bureau that provided the report.
- **Your right to a free copy of your credit report** (within 60 days of denial).

If you qualify for a loan but receive a high interest rate due to your credit score, lenders must disclose your score and explain why you didn't receive better terms.

HOW CAN POOR CREDIT AFFECT A JOB SEARCH?

Bad credit can limit job opportunities, especially for positions in finance, security, or management. However, new state-level laws have restricted employer credit checks in many places.

- Employers in some states (like California, New York, and Illinois) can no longer use credit reports for hiring decisions unless the job involves handling large sums of money or sensitive financial data.
- Employers must get your written permission before checking your credit report.
- If denied employment due to your credit, you must receive a copy of the report before the decision is final.

According to the **Fair Credit Reporting Act** (FCRA), which is enforced by the Federal Trade Commission (FTC) and your state Attorney General, an employer must get your permission to look at your credit report. If you don't get a job because of information in your report, the employer must give you written instructions on how to challenge the accuracy of the information in your report. Accurate negative information can stay on your report for seven years; bankruptcy may be reported for 10 years.

GETTING BUSINESS CREDIT

Whether planning to start your own business or expand the one you own, you may be in the market for credit. When you shop for a loan or line of credit, remember that the law protects you against discrimination. The **Equal Credit Opportunity Act** (ECOA) prohibits creditors from denying you a loan based on reasons other than credit-worthiness.

> ***The Federal Trade Commission (FTC) wants you to know that you cannot be denied business credit on the basis of your race, color, religion, national origin, sex, marital status, or age or that of your customers.***

For example, if you request a loan to open a store, a creditor can t deny your application based on your race or your customers.

If your application for personal or business credit is rejected, you can find out why. You must submit a written request for the reasons within 60 days of the denial. The creditor must give you the specific reasons in writing within 30 days of your request. If you don t agree with the reasons, consider discussing your concerns with the lender; you may be able to resolve the issues.

If your business is small (less than $1 million in gross revenues), the lender must keep records of your credit application for one year after telling you of the credit decision. If your business grosses more than $1 million, the lender has to keep your records on file for only 60 days after denying you credit. You can ask that your records be kept longer and you can ask for a written statement of the reasons for denial.

Additional ways to better your chances of getting business credit are:

- **Establish a Business Credit Profile:** Register for a DUNS Number (via Dun & Bradstreet).
- **Use Business Credit Cards:** Banks like Chase, Amex, and Capital One now offer business credit cards that don't require a personal guarantee.
- **Check Business Credit Reports:** Unlike personal credit, business credit is public record and can be checked via Dun & Bradstreet, Experian Business, or Equifax Business.

FIVE TIPS FOR GETTING THE MOST OUT OF YOUR CREDIT CARD

❒ **Pay on time.** Paying your credit card account on time helps you avoid late fees as well as penalty interest rates applied to your account, and helps you maintain a good credit record. A good credit record leads to a higher credit score, which helps you qualify for lower interest rates. Know the date your payment is due. If your bill is due at an inconvenient time of the month--for example, if it's due on the 10th and you get paid on the 15th, contact your credit card company to see if they will change your billing cycle to fit your cash flow.

❒ **Stay below your credit limit.** If you go over your credit limit on your card, your card issuer could charge a fee and increase your interest rate to a higher penalty rate. To avoid this, keep a record of your spending or check your balance online. Also, be aware that some merchants (for example, hotel and car rental companies) put a "hold" on your credit card based on their estimate of the amount you will charge. This can reduce your available credit until the final charge is processed. See *Credit and Debit Card Blocking.*

- ❒ **Avoid unnecessary fees.** Credit card companies not only charge late payment and over-the-limit fees, but also fees for cash advances, transferring balances, and having a payment returned. Some companies charge a fee when you pay your bill by phone. Pay attention to the transactions that trigger these fees. If you need a cash advance, withdraw enough so that you don't have to take a second cash advance--and incur a second fee--later in the month. Read your credit card agreement to learn more about the fees that your credit card company charges. For more information see "*What are the fees?*"

- ❒ **Pay more than the minimum payment.** If you can't pay your balance in full each month, try to pay as much of the total as you can. Over time, you'll pay less in interest charges--money that you will be able to spend on other things, and you'll pay off your balance sooner.

- ❒ **Watch for changes in the terms of your account.** Credit card companies can change the terms and conditions of your account. They will send you advance notices about changes in fees, interest rates, billing, and other features. By reading these "change in terms" notices, you can decide whether you want to change the way you use the card. For example, if cash advance fees increase, you may decide to use a different card for cash advances. If you have a card with a variable rate or if you have an introductory rate that is ending, be aware that credit card companies are not required to send you a notice about raising your interest rate. Interest rates are listed on your monthly bill. Read your bill carefully and take note of any changes.

FIVE TIPS FOR IMPROVING YOUR CREDIT SCORE

1. **Get copies of your credit report, then make sure the information is correct.**

Go to *www.annualcreditreport.com*. This is the only authorized online source for a free credit report. Under federal law, you can get a free report from each of the three national credit reporting companies every 12 months.

You can also call 877-322-8228 or complete the Annual Credit Report Request Form at *www.ftc.gov/bcp/conline/include/requestformfinal.pdf* and mail it to

Annual Credit Report Request Service
P.O. Box 105281
Atlanta, GA 30348-5281

2. **Pay your bills on time.**

One of the most important things you can do to improve your credit score is pay your bills by the due date. You can set up automatic payments from your bank account to help you pay on time, but be sure you have enough money in your account to avoid overdraft fees.

3. **Understand how your credit score is determined.**

Your credit score is usually based on the answers to these questions:

- **Do you pay your bills on time?** The answer to this question is very important. If you have paid bills late, have had an account referred to a collection agency, or have ever declared bankruptcy, this history will show up in your credit report.
- **What is your outstanding debt?** Many scoring models compare the amount of debt you have and your credit limits. If the amount you owe is close to

your credit limit, it is likely to have a negative effect on your score.

- **How long is your credit history?** A short credit history may have a negative effect on your score, but a short history can be offset by other factors, such as timely payments and low balances.
- **Have you applied for new credit recently?** If you have applied for too many new accounts recently, that may negatively affect your score. However, if you request a copy of your own credit report, or if creditors are monitoring your account or looking at credit reports to make prescreened credit offers, these inquiries about your credit history are not counted as applications for credit.
- **How many and what types of credit accounts do you have?** Many credit-scoring models consider the number and type of credit accounts you have. A mix of installment loans and credit cards may improve your score. However, too many finance company accounts or credit cards might hurt your score.

To learn more, see the Federal Trade Commission's publication on credit scoring.

4. **Learn the legal steps you must take to improve your credit report.**

The Federal Trade Commission's "Building a Better Credit Report" has information on correcting errors in your report, tips on dealing with debt and avoiding scams--and more.

5. **Beware of credit-repair scams.**

Consult the National Foundation for Credit Counseling the Federal Trade Commission and the Better Business Bureau when you have questions about a credit counseling or credit repair company.

THE NATIONAL FOUNDATION FOR CREDIT COUNSELING

National Foundation for Consumer Credit (NFCC) is the nation's largest and longest serving national nonprofit credit counseling network. The NFCC is the parent group for Consumer Credit Counseling Service.

It sets standards for

- Quality credit counseling
- Debt reduction services and
- Assistance in setting up a realistic personal budget.
- Possible negotiations with creditors to make arrangements for reduced payments on bills and
- Assistance in planning for future expenses.
- Helps individuals with credit concerns find helpful counseling in their areas

RESOURCES

Office of the Comptroller of the Currency (OCC)
Customer Assistance Group
1301 McKinney Street, Suite 3450
Houston, TX 77010
Phone: 800-613-6743
Fax: 713-336-4301
E-mail: *customer.assistance@occ.treas.gov*

The OCC deals chiefly with national banks and national-bank-owned mortgage companies.

Office of Thrift Supervision (OTS)
Consumer Affairs
1700 G Street NW Washington, DC 20552
Phone: 800-842-6929
TDD: 800-877-8339
The OTS deals chiefly with savings and loan associations.

National Credit Union Administration (NCUA)

Office of Public and Congressional Affairs
1775 Duke Street
Alexandria, VA 22314
Phone: 800-755-1030
Fax: 703-518-6409
E-mail: *consumerassistance@ncua.gov*

NCUA deals solely with federally-chartered credit unions. For state- chartered credit unions, contact the regulatory agency in the state in which the credit union is chartered.

Small Business Administration (SBA)
Consumer Affairs
409 3rd Street SW
Washington, DC 20416
Phone: 800-U-ASK-SBA (827-5722)
TDD: 704-344-6640
E-mail: *answerdesk@sba.gov*

Federal Trade Commission (FTC)
Consumer Response Center
240 600 Pennsylvania Avenue NW
Washington, DC 20580
Phone: 877-FTC-HELP (382-4357)
TDD: 866-653-4261
Also see *Fighting Back Against Identity Theft.*

Finance companies, stores, auto dealers, mortgage companies, and other lenders, and credit bureaus.

U.S. Department of Justice (DOJ)
950 Pennsylvania Avenue NW
Washington, DC 20530
Phone: 202-514-3301

Complaints involving housing discrimination and other matters as well as fair lending and fair housing issues.

Department of Housing and Urban Development
(HUD)
Office of Fair Housing and Equal Opportunity
451 7th Street SW
Washington, DC 20410
Phone: 800-669-9777
TDD: 800-927-9275

Securities and Exchange Commission (SEC)
Complaint Center
100 F Street NE
Washington, DC 20549
Phone: 202-551-6551
Fax: 202-772-9295

Brokerage firms, mutual fund companies, and investment advisers.

6

BOUND FOR GOOD CREDIT

This section discusses:

- ❐ **Self-help**
- ❐ **Developing a budget**
- ❐ **Contacting Your Creditors**
- ❐ **Dealing with Debt Collectors**
- ❐ **Credit Counseling**
- ❐ **Debt Repayment Plans**
- ❐ **Automobile and Home Loans**
- ❐ **Debt Consolidation**
- ❐ **Bankruptcy**
- ❐ **Chapter 13 Bankruptcy**
- ❐ **Chapter 7 Bankruptcy**
- ❐ **Damage Control**

Debt got you down? You're not alone. Consumer debt is at an all-time high. Whether your debt dilemma is the result of illness, unemployment, or overspending, it can seem overwhelming. Don't despair. Legal alternatives can help you regain your financial foothold.

SELF HELP

Developing a Budget

The first step toward taking control of your financial situation is to do a realistic assessment of how much money comes in and how much money you spend. Start by listing your income from all sources. Then, list your "fixed" expenses--those that are the same each month, such as mortgage payments or rent, car payments, or insurance premiums. Next, list the expenses that vary, such as entertainment, recreation, or clothing. Writing down all your expenses--even those that seem insignificant--is a helpful way to track your spending patterns, identify the expenses that are necessary, and prioritize the rest. The goal is to make sure you can make ends meet on the basics: housing, food, health care, insurance, and education.

Your public library and online resources, such as personal finance websites and budgeting apps, provide information about budgeting and money management techniques. Low cost budget counseling services that can help you analyze your income and expenses and develop budget and spending plans also are available in most communities. Search online or contact your local bank, consumer protection office, or reputable financial counseling organizations for information. In addition, many universities, military bases, credit unions, and housing authorities operate nonprofit counseling programs.

Contacting Your Creditors

Contact your creditors immediately if you are having trouble making ends meet. Tell them why it's difficult for you, and try to work out a modified payment plan that reduces your payments to a more manageable level. Don't wait until your accounts have been turned over to a debt collector. At that point, the creditors have given up on you.

Dealing with Debt Collectors

The **Fair Debt Collection Practices Act** is the federal law that dictates how and when a debt collector may contact you. A debt collector may not call you before 8 a.m., after 9 p.m., or at work if the collector knows that your employer doesn't approve of the calls. Collectors may not harass you, make false statements, or use unfair practices when they try to collect a debt. Debt collectors must honor a written request from you to cease further contact. You can also submit this request through email or online dispute portals provided by major collection agencies.

CREDIT COUNSELING

Debt Repayment Plans

If you aren't disciplined enough to create a workable budget and stick to it, can't work out a repayment plan with your creditors, or can't keep track of mounting bills, consider contacting a credit counseling service. Your creditors may be willing to accept reduced payments or adjust interest rates if you enter a debt repayment plan through a reputable nonprofit credit counseling organization. In these plans, you deposit money each month with the credit counseling service. Your deposits are used to pay your creditors according to a payment schedule developed by the counselor. As part of the repayment plan, you may have to agree not to apply for—or use—any additional credit while you're participating in the program.

A successful repayment plan requires you to make regular, timely payments, and could take 48 months or longer to complete. Ask the credit counseling service for an estimate of the time it will take to complete the plan. Some nonprofit credit counseling services offer free or low-cost debt management plans, while others may charge monthly fees that could add up over time. Be sure to research and verify their legitimacy through organizations like the **National Foundation for Credit Counseling** (**NFCC**)—*www.nfcc.org*—or the **Financial Counseling Association of America** (**FCAA**)—*www.fcaa.org*. Some credit counseling services are funded, in part, by contributions from creditors.

While a debt repayment plan can eliminate much of the stress that comes from dealing with creditors and overdue bills, it does not mean you can forget about your debts. You still are responsible for paying any creditors whose debts are not included in the plan. You are responsible for reviewing monthly statements from your creditors to make sure your payments have been received. If your repayment plan depends on your creditors agreeing to lower or eliminate interest and finance charges, or waive late fees, you are responsible for making sure these concessions are reflected on your statements.

A debt repayment plan does not erase your credit history. Under the Fair Credit Reporting Act, accurate information about your accounts can stay on your credit report for up to seven years. In addition, your creditors will continue to report information about accounts that are handled through a debt repayment plan. For example, creditors may report that an account is in financial counseling, that payments may have been late or missed altogether, or that there are write-offs or other concessions. A demonstrated pattern of timely payments will help you obtain credit in the future.

Auto and Home Loans

Debt repayment plans usually cover unsecured debt. Your auto and home loan, which are considered secured debt, may not be included. You must continue to make payments to these creditors directly.

Most automobile financing agreements allow a creditor to repossess your car any time you're in default. No notice is required. If your car is repossessed, you may have to pay the full balance due on the loan, as well as towing and storage costs, to get it back. If you can't do this, the creditor may sell the car. If you see default approaching, you may be better off selling the car yourself and paying off the debt—you would avoid the added costs of repossession and a negative entry on your credit report.

If you fall behind on your mortgage, contact your lender immediately to avoid foreclosure. Most lenders are willing to work with you if they believe you're acting in good faith and the situation is temporary. Some lenders may reduce or suspend your payments for a short time. When you resume regular payments, though, you may have to pay an additional amount toward the past due total. Other lenders may agree to change the terms of the mortgage by extending the repayment period to reduce the monthly debt. Ask whether additional fees would be assessed for these changes, and calculate how much they total in the long term.

If you and your lender cannot work out a plan, contact a housing counseling agency. Some agencies limit their counseling services to homeowners with FHA mortgages, but many offer free help to any homeowner who's having trouble making mortgage payments. **Visit the U.S. Department of Housing and Urban Development** (**HUD**) website—*www.hud.gov*—to locate approved housing counseling agencies in your area.

DEBT CONSOLIDATION

You may be able to lower your cost of credit by consolidating your debt through a second mortgage or a home equity line of credit (HELOC). Think carefully before taking this on. These loans require your home as collateral. If you can't make payments—or if payments are late—you risk foreclosure. Explore alternatives such as—

- personal loans,
- balance transfer credit cards, or
- working with credit unions

—before using your home as collateral.

The costs of these consolidation loans can add up. In addition to interest on the loan, you pay "points." Typically, one point is equal to one percent of the amount you borrow. Still, these loans may provide certain tax advantages that are not available with other kinds of credit.

BANKRUPTCY

Personal bankruptcy generally is considered the debt management option of last resort because the results are long-lasting and far-reaching. A bankruptcy stays on your credit report for 10 years, making it difficult to acquire credit, buy a home, get life insurance, or sometimes, get a job. However, it is a legal procedure that offers a fresh start for people who can't satisfy their debts.

There are two kinds of personal bankruptcy:

- **Chapter 13**
- **Chapter 7**

Each must be filed in federal court. As of 2025, the filing fees for bankruptcy are $338 for Chapter 7 and $313 for Chapter 13, though these amounts may change. Check the U.S. Courts website—*www.uscourts.gov*—for updated fees.

Chapter 13

Also known as reorganization, Chapter 13 allows debtors to keep property, like a mortgaged house or a car, that they otherwise might lose. Reorganization may allow you to pay off a default during a three-to-five-year period, rather than surrender any property.

Chapter 7

Known as straight bankruptcy, Chapter 7 involves liquidation of all assets that are not exempt in your state. Exempt property may include work-related tools and basic household furnishings. Some of your property may be sold by a court-appointed official or turned over to your creditors. You can file for Chapter 7 only once every six years.

Both types of bankruptcy may get rid of unsecured debts and stop foreclosures, repossessions, garnishments, utility shutoffs, and debt collection activities. Both also provide exemptions that allow people to keep certain assets, although exemption amounts vary among states. Note that personal bankruptcy usually does not erase child support, alimony, fines, taxes, and some student loan obligations. And unless you have an acceptable plan to catch up on your debt under Chapter 13, bankruptcy usually does not allow you to keep property when your creditor has an unpaid mortgage or lien on it.

DAMAGE CONTROL

Turning to a business that offers help in solving debt problems may seem like a reasonable solution when your bills become unmanageable. Be cautious. Before you do business with any company, check it out with your local consumer protection agency or the Better Business Bureau in the company's location.

Some businesses that offer debt counseling and reorganization plans may charge high fees and fail to follow through on the services they sell. Others may misrepresent the terms of a debt consolidation loan, failing either to explain certain costs or to mention that you're signing over your home as collateral. Businesses advertising voluntary debt reorganization plans may not explain that the plan is a Chapter 13 bankruptcy, tell you everything that's involved, or help you through what can be a complex and lengthy legal process.

In addition, some companies guarantee you a loan if you pay a fee in advance. The fee may range from $100 to several hundred dollars. Resist the temptation to follow up on advance-fee loan guarantees. They may be illegal. Many legitimate creditors offer extensions of credit through telemarketing and require an application or appraisal fee in advance. But legitimate creditors never guarantee that the consumer will get the loan—or even represent that it is likely. Under the federal **Telemarketing Sales Rule**, a seller or telemarketer who guarantees or represents a high likelihood of your getting a loan or some other extension of credit may not ask for or receive payment until you've received the loan.

You also should avoid credit repair clinics. Many online and in-person credit repair services make bold claims about erasing bad credit for a fee. Be cautious—under the **Credit Repair Organizations Act (CROA)**, no company can legally remove accurate negative information from your credit report. They don't deliver. What's more, they can't deliver—they can't do anything for you that you can't do for yourself. After you pay them hundreds—or even thousands—of dollars in up-front fees, they can do nothing to improve your credit report. Indeed, many simply vanish with your money.

> ***Only time and a conscientious effort to repay your debts will improve your credit report. If you're thinking about getting help to stabilize your financial situation, be cautious.***

Find out what services the business provides and what it charges. Don't rely on oral promises. Get everything in writing. Research companies through your state attorney general's office, consumer protection agency, or the Better Business Bureau (*www.bbb.org*). They may be able to tell you whether other consumers have registered complaints about the business.

MORE DEBT RELIEF OPTIONS

In addition to traditional credit counseling, some consumers explore AI-driven budgeting tools and debt settlement companies. However, debt settlement can impact credit scores and may come with high fees, so thorough research is necessary.

Apps such as Mint, YNAB (You Need a Budget), and EveryDollar help consumers track spending, set financial goals, and automate debt repayment strategies.

7

CREDIT AND YOUR CONSUMER RIGHTS

A good credit rating is very important. Businesses inspect your credit history when they evaluate your applications for credit, insurance, employment, and even leases. Based on your credit payment history, businesses can choose to grant or deny you credit provided you receive fair and equal treatment. Sometimes, things happen that can cause credit problems: a temporary loss of income, an illness, even a computer error. Solving credit problems may take time and patience, but it doesn't have to be an ordeal.

The Federal Trade Commission (FTC) enforces credit laws that protect your right to obtain, use, and maintain credit. These laws do not guarantee that everyone will receive credit. Instead, the credit laws protect your rights by requiring businesses to give all consumers a fair and equal opportunity to receive credit and to resolve disputes over credit errors.

YOUR CREDIT REPORT

Your credit payment history is recorded in a file or report. These files or reports are maintained and sold by **consumer reporting agencies** (CRAs). The most well-known CRAs are the three major credit bureaus: Experian, Equifax, and TransUnion. You have a credit record on file at a credit bureau if you have ever applied for a credit or charge account, a personal loan, insurance, or a job. Your credit record contains information about your income, debts, and credit payment history. It also indicates whether you have been sued, arrested, or have filed for bankruptcy.

You are entitled to one free credit report per year from each major credit bureau through *www.annualcreditreport.*

com. Some banks and financial apps, such as Credit Karma and Experian Boost, offer free access to credit reports more frequently.

The **Fair Credit Reporting Act (FCRA)** is designed to help ensure that CRAs furnish correct and complete information to businesses to use when evaluating your application.

Your rights under the Fair Credit Reporting Act:

- You have the right to receive a free credit report every 12 months from each bureau. Additionally, some states allow for extra free reports, and the federal government now provides free weekly access to credit reports through 2026.
- The copy of your report must contain all of the information in your file at the time of your request.
- You have the right to know the name of anyone who received your credit report in the last year for most purposes or in the last two years for employment purposes.
- Any company that denies your application must supply the name and address of the CRA they contacted, provided the denial was based on information given by the CRA.
- You have the right to a free copy of your credit report when your application is denied because of information supplied by a CRA. Your request must be made within 60 days of receiving your denial notice.
- If you contest the completeness or accuracy of information in your report, you should file a dispute with the CRA and with the company that furnished the information to the CRA.
- Both the CRA and the furnisher of information are legally obligated to reinvestigate your dispute.

- You have a right to add a summary explanation to your credit report if your dispute is not resolved to your satisfaction.

YOUR CREDIT APPLICATION

When creditors evaluate a credit application, they cannot lawfully engage in discriminatory practices.

The **Equal Credit Opportunity Act (ECOA)** prohibits credit discrimination on the basis of sex, race, marital status, religion, national origin, age, or receipt of public assistance. Creditors may ask for this information (except religion) in certain situations, but may not use it to discriminate when deciding whether to grant you credit.

The ECOA protects consumers who deal with companies that regularly extend credit, including banks, small loan and finance companies, retail and department stores, credit card companies, and credit unions. Everyone who participates in the decision to grant credit, including real estate brokers who arrange financing, must follow this law. Small business owners applying for credit are also protected by this law, ensuring they are evaluated fairly when seeking funding for their business.

YOUR RIGHTS UNDER THE EQUAL CREDIT OPPORTUNITY ACT

- You cannot be denied credit based on your race, sex, marital status, religion, age, national origin, or receipt of public assistance.
- You have the right to have reliable public assistance considered in the same manner as other income.
- If you are denied credit, you have a legal right to know why.

YOUR CREDIT BILLING AND ELECTRONIC FUND TRANSFER STATEMENTS

It is important to check credit billing and electronic fund transfer account statements regularly. These documents may contain mistakes that could damage your credit status or reflect improper charges or transfers. If you find an error or discrepancy, notify the company and contest the error immediately. The Fair Credit Billing Act (FCBA) and Electronic Fund Transfer Act (EFTA) establish procedures for resolving mistakes on credit billing and electronic fund transfer account statements, including:

- charges or electronic fund transfers that you--or anyone you have authorized to use your account--have not made;
- charges or electronic fund transfers that are incorrectly identified or show the wrong amount or date;
- computation or similar errors;
- failure to reflect payments, credits, or electronic fund transfers properly;
- not mailing or delivering credit billing statements to your current address, as long as that address was received by the creditor in writing at least 20 days before the billing period ended;
- charges or electronic fund transfers for which you request an explanation or documentation, due to a possible error.

The FCBA generally applies only to "open end" credit accounts—credit cards, revolving charge accounts (such as department store accounts), and overdraft checking accounts. It does not apply to loans or credit sales that are paid according to a fixed schedule until the entire amount is paid back, such as an automobile loan. The EFTA applies to electronic fund transfers, such as those involving automatic teller machines (ATMs), point-of-sale debit transactions, and other electronic banking transactions.

YOUR DEBTS AND DEBT COLLECTORS

You are responsible for your debts. If you fall behind in paying your creditors or an error is made on your account, you may be contacted by a "debt collector." A debt collector is any person, other than the creditor, who regularly collects debts owed to others. This includes lawyers who collect debts. You have the right to be treated fairly by debt collectors.

The **Fair Debt Collection Practices Act** (FDCPA) applies to personal, family, and household debts. This includes money owed for the purchase of a car, for medical care, or for charge accounts. The FDCPA prohibits debt collectors from engaging in unfair, deceptive, or abusive practices while collecting these debts.

Your rights under the Fair Debt Collection Practices Act:

- Debt collectors can only contact you between 8 a.m. and 9 p.m., but many states have additional restrictions on collection calls. Check your state laws for additional protections.
- Debt collectors may not contact you at work if they know your employer disapproves.
- Debt collectors may not harass, oppress, or abuse you.
- Debt collectors may not lie when collecting debts, such as falsely implying that you have committed a crime.
- Debt collectors must identify themselves to you on the phone.
- You can request in writing that a debt collector stops contacting you. However, this does not erase the debt, and legal actions may still follow if you owe the balance.

SOLVING YOUR CREDIT PROBLEMS

Your credit report influences your purchasing power, as well as your chances to get a job, rent or buy an apartment or a house, and buy insurance. A history of timely credit payments helps you get additional credit. Accurate negative information can stay on your report for seven years. A bankruptcy can stay on your report for 10 years. If you are having problems paying your bills, contact your creditors at once. Try to work out a modified payment plan with them that reduces your payments to a more manageable level. Don't wait until your account has been turned over to a debt collector.

Some credit repair companies and credit reporting agencies might give you copies of forms you can use to file your dispute information with the credit reporting agency. Be sure to ask about these. They could be a good help when preparing your complaint.

Here are some additional tips for solving credit problems:

- **If you want to contest a credit report, bill or credit denial, contact the appropriate company in writing and send it "return receipt requested."** Many credit bureaus now allow disputes to be filed online, making the process faster. If you choose to dispute online, ensure you keep screenshots and reference numbers for documentation.
- **When you contest a billing error, include your name, account number, the dollar amount in question, and the reason you believe the bill is wrong.**
- **If in doubt, request written verification of a debt.**
- **Keep all your original documents, especially receipts, sales slips, and billing statements.** You will need them if you dispute a credit bill or report. Send

copies only. It may take more than one letter to correct problems.

- **Be skeptical of businesses that offer instant solutions to credit problems.**
- **Be persistent.** Resolving credit problems can take time and effort.
- **There is nothing that a credit repair company can do for you—for a fee—that you cannot do for yourself for little or no cost.**
- **If you can't resolve your credit problems yourself or if you need help, you may want to contact a credit counseling service.** Nonprofit organizations in every state counsel consumers in debt and they try to arrange realistic repayment plans. They also can help you set up a realistic budget. These services usually are offered at little or no cost.
- **Universities, military bases, credit unions, and housing authorities also may offer low- or no-cost credit counseling programs.** Check the white pages of your telephone directory for a service near you.

8

HOW TO DISPUTE CREDIT CARD ERRORS

Your credit report—a type of consumer report—contains information about where you work and live and how you pay your bills. It also may show whether you've been sued or arrested or have filed for bankruptcy. Companies called consumer reporting agencies (CRAs) or credit bureaus compile and sell your credit report to businesses. Because businesses use this information to evaluate your applications for credit, insurance, employment, and other purposes allowed by the Fair Credit Reporting Act (FCRA), it's important that the information in your report is complete and accurate.

Some financial advisors suggest that you periodically review your credit report for inaccuracies or omissions. This could be especially important if you're considering making a major purchase, such as buying a home. Checking in advance on the accuracy of information in your credit file could speed the credit-granting process.

GETTING YOUR CREDIT REPORT

If you've been denied credit, insurance, or employment because of information supplied by a CRA, the FCRA says the company you applied to must give you the CRA's name, address, and telephone number. If you contact the agency for a copy of your report within 60 days of receiving a denial notice, the report is free. In addition, you're entitled to one free copy of your report a year if you certify in writing that

1. you're unemployed and plan to look for a job within 60 days,
2. you're on welfare, or

3. your report is inaccurate because of fraud.

Otherwise, a CRA may charge a fee for additional copies of your report, though many banks and credit card issuers offer free access to credit scores and reports through their online portals.

CORRECTING ERRORS

Under the FCRA, both the CRA and the organization that provided the information to the CRA, such as a bank or credit card company, have responsibilities for correcting inaccurate or incomplete information in your report. To protect all your rights under the law, contact both the CRA and the information provider.

First, tell the CRA in writing what information you believe is inaccurate. Include copies (NOT originals) of documents that support your position. In addition to providing your complete name and address, your letter should clearly identify each item in your report you dispute, state the facts and explain why you dispute the information, and request deletion or correction. You may want to enclose a copy of your report with the items in question circled. You can send your letter by certified mail, return receipt requested, or file disputes online through the credit bureau's website for faster processing. Keep copies of your dispute letter and enclosures.

CRAs must reinvestigate the items in question—usually within 30 days—unless they consider your dispute frivolous. They also must forward all relevant data you provide about the dispute to the information provider. After the information provider receives notice of a dispute from the CRA, it must investigate, review all relevant information provided by the CRA, and report the results to the CRA. If the information provider finds the disputed information to be inaccurate, it must notify all nationwide CRAs so they can correct this information in your file. Disputed information that cannot be verified must be deleted from your file.

If your report contains erroneous information, the CRA must correct it. If an item is incomplete, the CRA must complete it. For example, if your file showed that you were late making payments, but failed to show that you were no longer delinquent, the CRA must show that you're current.

If your file shows an account that belongs only to another person, the CRA must delete it.

When the reinvestigation is complete, the CRA must give you the written results and a free copy of your report if the dispute results in a change. If an item is changed or removed, the CRA cannot put the disputed information back in your file unless the information provider verifies its accuracy and completeness, and the CRA gives you a written notice that includes the name, address, and phone number of the provider.

Also, if you request, the CRA must send notices of corrections to anyone who received your report in the past six months. Job applicants can have a corrected copy of their report sent to anyone who received a copy during the past two years for employment purposes. If a reinvestigation does not resolve your dispute, ask the CRA to include your statement of the dispute in your file and in future reports.

Second, in addition to writing to the CRA, tell the creditor or other information provider in writing that you dispute an item. Include copies (*not* originals) of documents that support your position. Many providers specify an address for disputes. If the provider then reports the item to any CRA, it must include a notice of your dispute. In addition, if you are correct—that is, if the disputed information is not accurate—the information provider may not use it again.

ACCURATE NEGATIVE INFORMATION

When negative information in your report is accurate, only the passage of time can assure its removal. Accurate negative information can generally stay on your report for 7 years.

There are certain exceptions:

- Information about criminal convictions may be reported without any time limitation.
- Bankruptcy information may be reported for 10 years.
- Credit information reported in response to an application for a job with a salary of more than $75,000 has no time limit.
- Credit information reported because of an application for more than $150,000 worth of credit or life insurance has no time limit.
- Information about a lawsuit or an unpaid judgment against you can be reported for seven years or until the statute of limitations runs out, whichever is longer.
- Criminal convictions can be reported without any time limit.
- Some lenders now use alternative credit data, such as utility payments and rent history, to evaluate creditworthiness. If you have a limited credit history, consider services that report these payments to credit bureaus.

ADDING ACCOUNTS TO YOUR FILE

Your credit file may not reflect all your credit accounts. Although most national department store and all-purpose bank credit card accounts will be included in your file, not all creditors supply information to CRAs: Some travel, entertainment, gasoline card companies, local retailers, and credit unions are among those creditors that don't.

If you've been told you were denied credit because of an "insufficient credit file" or "no credit file" and you have accounts with creditors that don't appear in your credit file, ask the CRA to add this information to future reports. Although they are not required to do so, many CRAs will add verifiable accounts for a fee. You should, however, understand that if these creditors do not report to the CRA on a regular basis, these added items will not be updated in your file.

Some financial services allow you to link your rent, utility, and subscription payments to your credit file to help build credit history. Services like Experian Boost and eCredable Lift can report alternative financial data to improve your credit score.

SAMPLE DISPUTE LETTER

The following are sample letters that may guide you in preparing your own credit dispute letter if you need one. The first is an example of a letter requesting that inaccurate information be removed from a credit report.

As stated earlier, when you prepare a dispute letter, include any documents that prove or support the points you make in your letter. You might include credit card statements, letters from creditors stating that your accounts are in good standing, canceled checks showing on- time payments, paid off loans—in short, anything that can show that information your credit report is wrong. You can also document any negative consequences of the erroneous information, such as being turned down for credit because of the bad information.

Many credit bureaus now allow disputes to be filed online or via mobile apps, often resolving issues faster than traditional mail-in requests.

Note: Portions of text in square brackets are instructions to help you prepare more effective dispute letters. Be sure to remove these statements from your actual letters.

Your Name
123 Your Street Address
Your City, ST 01234
Date

The Credit Bureau [Experian, Equifax or TransUnion]
Bureau Address
Anytown, State 56789

Dear [Credit Bureau],

This letter is a formal complaint concerning inaccurate credit information in my credit report.

The inclusion of the inaccurate information in my report has had a damaging effect on my good credit standing. As you know, credit reporting laws attempt to ensure that bureaus report only accurate credit information. No doubt the inclusion of this inaccurate information is a mistake on either your or the reporting creditor's part. Because of the mistakes on my credit report, I have been wrongfully denied credit recently for a [insert credit type for which you were denied here], which was highly distressing to me and my family.

Along with this letter, I've included supporting proof that shows my dispute is valid and that the bad data needs to be removed as soon as possible.

The following information therefore needs to be verified and deleted from the report as soon as possible:
[CREDITOR AGENCY, ACCOUNT NUMBER]

Please delete the following information as quickly as possible:

[full text and numerical data constituting the inaccurate information]

Sincerely,

Your signature
Your Name
SSN# 123-45-6789
Attachment included.

9

CONSUMER HANDBOOK OF CREDIT PROTECTION LAWS

The Consumer Credit Protection Act of 1968—which introduced **Truth in Lending** (**TILA**)—was a landmark law that set the foundation for modern credit transparency. Today, with the rise of digital lending, mobile banking, and fintech platforms, additional regulations have been introduced to ensure fair and accurate disclosures. Borrowers now receive loan cost information not only in printed documents but also electronically through banking apps, emails, and online portals, making credit comparison easier than ever.

Since 1968, credit protections have multiplied rapidly. The concepts of "fair" and "equal" credit have been written into laws that outlaw unfair discrimination in credit transactions; require that consumers be told the reason when credit is denied; let borrowers find out about their credit records; and set up a way to settle billing disputes.

Each law was meant to reduce the problems and confusion surrounding consumer credit which, as it became more widely used in our economy, also grew more complex. Together, these laws set a standard for how individuals are to be treated in their financial dealings.

The laws say, for instance, that you cannot be turned down for a credit card just because you're a single woman; that you can limit your risk if a credit card is lost or stolen; that you can straighten out errors in your monthly bill without damage to your credit rating; and that you won't find credit shut off just because you've reached the age of 65.

But, let the buyer be aware! It is important to know your rights and how to use them. This handbook explains how the consumer credit laws can help you shop for credit, apply for it, keep up your credit standing, and—if need be—complain about an unfair deal. It explains what you should look for when using credit and what creditors look for before extending it. It also points out the laws' solutions to discriminatory practices that have made it difficult for women and minorities to get credit in the past.

THE COST OF CREDIT

Shopping is the First Step

You get credit by promising to pay in the future for something you receive in the present. Credit is a convenience. It lets you charge a meal on your credit card, pay for an appliance on the installment plan, take out a loan to buy a house, or pay for schooling or vacations. With credit, you can enjoy your purchase while you're paying for it—or you can make a purchase when you're lacking ready cash.

But there are strings attached to credit too. It usually costs something. And of course what is borrowed must be paid back.

If you are thinking of borrowing or opening a credit account, your first step should be to figure out how much it will cost you and whether you can afford it. Then you should shop around for the best terms.

What Laws Apply?

Two major laws continue to protect borrowers:

- **Truth in Lending Act (TILA)** ensures that lenders disclose the true cost of credit, including interest rates and fees. Today, TILA applies not only to traditional loans but also to digital lenders, Buy Now, Pay Later (BNPL) services, and mobile-based credit options.

- **Consumer leasing disclosures** require transparency in lease agreements, whether for vehicles, electronics, or subscription-based services, allowing consumers to compare leasing costs against outright purchases.

The Finance Charge and Annual Percentage Rate (APR)

Credit costs vary. By remembering two terms, you can compare credit prices from different sources. Under Truth in Lending, the creditor must tell you—in writing and before you sign any agreement—the finance charge and the annual percentage rate.

The **finance charge** is the total cost of borrowing, including interest, service fees, and any mandatory insurance. With the rise of fintech lending and peer-to-peer lending platforms, borrowers should also watch for origination fees, transaction fees, and early payment penalties, which can vary widely among online and traditional lenders.

For example, borrowing $100 for a year might cost you $10 in interest. If there were also a service charge of $1, the finance charge would be $11.

The **annual percentage rate** (APR) is the percentage cost (or relative cost) of credit on a yearly basis. This is your key to comparing costs, regardless of the amount of credit or how long you have to repay it:

Again, suppose you borrow $100 for one year and pay a finance charge of $10. If you can keep the entire $100 for the whole year and then pay back $110 at the end of the year, you are paying an APR of 10%. But, if you repay the $100 and finance charge (a total of $110) in twelve equal monthly installments, you don't really get to use $100 for the whole year. In fact, you get to use less and less of that $100 each month. In this case, the $10 charge for credit amounts to an APR of 18%.

All creditors—banks, stores, car dealers, credit card companies, finance companies—must state the cost of their credit in terms of the finance charge and the APR. Federal law does not set interest rates or other credit charges, but it does require their disclosure so that you can compare credit costs. The law says these two pieces of information must be shown to you before you sign a credit contract or before you use a credit card.

A Comparison

Even when you understand the terms a creditor is offering, it's easy to underestimate the difference in dollars that different terms can make. Suppose you're buying a $7,500 car. You put $1,500 down, and need to borrow $6,000. Compare the three credit arrangements on the next page.

How do these choices stack up? The answer depends partly on what you need.

The lowest cost loan is available from Creditor A. If you were looking for lower monthly payments, you could get then by paying the loan off over a longer period of time. However, you would have to pay more in total costs. A loan from Creditor B—also at a 14 percent APR, but for four years—will add about $488 to your finance charge.

If that four-year loan were available only from Creditor C, the APR of 15 percent would add another $145 or so to your finance charges as compared with Creditor B.

Other terms, such as the size of the down payment, will also make a difference. Be sure to look at all the terms before you make your choice.

Cost of Open-end Credit

Open-end credit includes credit cards, Buy Now, Pay Later (BNPL) services, revolving credit accounts, home equity lines, and overdraft protection. Today, digital banking tools and apps such as Experian Boost, Credit Karma, and alternative credit scoring models are influencing how lenders assess your creditworthiness. Open-end credit can be used again and again, generally until you reach a certain prearranged borrowing limit. Truth in Lending requires that open-end creditors tell you the terms of the credit plan so that you can shop and compare the costs involved.

When you're shopping for an open-end plan, the APR you're told represents only the periodic rate that you will be charged, figured on a yearly basis. For instance, a creditor that charges 1% percent interest each month would quote you an APR of 18%. Annual membership fees, transaction charges, and points, for example, are listed separately; they are not included in the APR. Keep this in mind and compare all the costs involved in the plans, not just the APR.

Creditors must tell you when finance charges begin on your account, so you know how much time you have to pay your bill before a finance charge is added. Creditors may give you a 25-day grace period, for example, to pay your balance in full before making you pay a finance charge.

Creditors also must tell you the method they use to figure the balance on which you pay a finance charge—the interest rate they charge is applied to this balance to come up with the finance charge. Creditors use a number of different methods to arrive at the balance. Study them carefully because they can significantly affect your finance charge.

Some creditors, for instance, take the amount you owed at the beginning of the billing cycle and subtract any payments you made during that cycle. Purchases are not counted. This is called the **adjusted balance method**.

Another is the **previous balance method**. Creditors simply use the amount owed at the beginning of the billing cycle to come up with the finance charge.

Under one of the most common methods—the **average daily balance method**—creditors add your balances for each day in the billing cycle and then divide that total by the number of days in the cycle. Payments made during the cycle are subtracted in arriving at the daily amounts and, depending on the plan, new purchases may or may not be included.

Under another method—the **two-cycle average daily balance method**—creditors use the average daily balances for two billing cycles to compute your finance charge. Again, payments will be taken into account in figuring the balances, but new purchases may or may not be included.

Be aware that the amount of the finance charge may vary considerably depending on the method used, even for the same pattern of purchases and payments.

If you receive a credit card offer or an application, the creditor must give you information about the APR and other important terms of the plan at that time. Likewise, with a home equity plan, information must be given to you with an application.

Truth in Lending does not set the rates or tell the creditor how to calculate finance charges—it only requires that the creditor tell you the method that it uses. You should ask for an explanation of any terms you don't understand.

LEASING COSTS AND TERMS

Leasing allows consumers to access cars, electronics, and even furniture for a fixed monthly payment without ownership. Subscription-based leasing models are growing, especially in the automotive and technology industries, where customers can swap devices or vehicles regularly. Digital lease management platforms now allow consumers to track, modify, or extend leases online. For instance, you might consider leasing furniture for an apartment you'll use only for a year.

The **Consumer Leasing law** requires leasing companies to give you the facts about the costs and terms of their contracts, to help you decide whether leasing is a good idea. The law applies to personal property leased to you for more than four months for personal, family, or household use. It covers, for example, long-term rentals of cars, furniture, and appliances, but not daily car rentals or leases for apartments.

Before you agree to a lease, the leasing company must give you a written statement of costs, including the amount of any security deposit, the amount of your monthly payments, and the amount you must pay for licensing, registration, taxes, and maintenance.

The company must also give you a written statement about terms, including any insurance you need, any guarantees, information about who is responsible for servicing the property, any standards for its wear and tear, and whether or not you have an option to buy the property.

Open-end Leases and Balloon Payments

Your costs will depend on whether you choose an open-end lease or a closed-end lease. Open-end leases usually mean lower monthly payments than closed-end leases, but you may owe a large extra payment—often called a balloon payment—based on the value of the property when you return it.

Suppose you lease a car under a three-year open-end lease. The leasing company estimates the car will be worth $4,000 after three years of normal use. If you bring back the car in a condition that makes it worth only $3,500, you may owe a balloon payment of $500.

The leasing company must tell you whether you may owe a balloon payment and how it will be calculated. You should also know that:

- You have the right to an independent appraisal of the property's worth at the end of the lease. You must pay the appraiser's fee, however.
- A balloon payment is usually limited to no more than three times the average monthly payment. If your monthly payment is $200, your balloon payment wouldn't be more than $600, unless, for example, the property has received more than average wear and tear (for instance, if you drove a car more than average mileage).

Closed-end leases usually have higher monthly payment than open-end leases, but there is no balloon payment at the end of the lease.

COSTS OF SETTLEMENT ON A HOUSE

A home purchase is often the largest financial decision a consumer will make. **The Real Estate Settlement Procedures Act (RESPA)** ensures transparency in mortgage transactions. Today, digital innovations such as e-mortgages, remote notarization, and AI-driven loan approvals are streamlining the home-buying process. Borrowers can now compare loan offers through online mortgage comparison tools, reducing the complexity of closing costs.

This event is called settlement or closing, and the law helps you shop for lower settlement costs.

NEW CREDIT TRENDS AND FINTECH INNOVATIONS

In addition to traditional credit protections, new financial technologies (fintech) are reshaping consumer borrowing.

- **Blockchain-based lending** is emerging, allowing users to secure loans using cryptocurrency as collateral.
- **AI-driven lending platforms** use alternative data points—such as utility payments, rental history, and subscription payments—to assess creditworthiness.
- **Digital-only banks and peer-to-peer lending services** offer credit options without traditional banking requirements, though terms can vary widely.

Consumers should carefully review the terms and disclosures of these modern credit services to ensure compliance with existing consumer protection laws.

10

APPLYING FOR CREDIT

When you're ready to apply for credit, you should know what creditors think is important in deciding whether you're creditworthy. You should also know what they cannot legally consider in their decisions.

WHAT LAW APPLIES?

The **Equal Credit Opportunity Act (ECOA)** ensures that all credit applicants are evaluated based on their financial qualifications, not on personal characteristics such as age, gender, race, or marital status.

WHAT CREDITORS LOOK FOR

The Three C's. Creditors look for an ability to repay debt and a willingness to do so—and sometimes for a little extra security to protect their loans. They speak of the three C's of credit-capacity, character, and collateral.

- **Capacity.** Can you repay the debt? Creditors ask for employment information: your occupation, how long you've worked, and how much you earn. They also want to know your expenses: how many dependents you have, whether you pay alimony or child support, and the amount of your other obligations.
- **Character.** Will you repay the debt? Creditors will look at your credit history and how much you owe, how often you borrow, whether you pay bills on time, and whether you live within your means. They also look for signs of stability: how long you've lived at your present address, whether you own or rent, and length of your present employment.
- **Collateral.** Is the creditor fully protected if you fail

to repay? Creditors want to know what you may have that could be used to back up or secure your loan, and what sources you have for repaying debt other than income, such as savings, investments, or property.

Creditors use different combinations of these facts in reaching their decisions. Credit standards vary among lenders. Some institutions maintain strict lending criteria, while others specialize in specific types of loans. Creditors also use different kinds of rating systems. Some rely strictly on their own instinct and experience. Others use a "credit-scoring" or statistical system to predict whether you're a good credit risk. They assign a certain number of points to each of the various characteristics that have proved to be reliable signs that a borrower will repay. Then, they rate you on this scale.

And so, different creditors may reach different conclusions based on the same set of facts. One may find you an acceptable risk, while another may deny you a loan.

INFORMATION THE CREDITOR CAN'T USE

The Equal Credit Opportunity Act does not guarantee that you will get credit. You must still pass the creditor's tests of creditworthiness. But the creditor must apply these tests fairly, impartially, and without discriminating against you on any of the following grounds: age, gender, marital status, race, color, religion, national origin, because you receive public income such as veterans benefits, welfare or Social Security, or because you exercise your rights under Federal credit laws such as filing a billing error notice with a creditor. This means that a creditor may not use any of those grounds as a reason to:

- discourage you from applying for a loan;
- refuse you a loan if you quality; or
- lend you money on terms different from those granted another person with similar income, expenses, credit history, and collateral.

Special Rules

Age. In the past, many older persons have complained about being denied credit just because they were over a certain age. Or when they retired, they often found their credit suddenly cut off or reduced. So the law is very specific about how a person's age may be used in credit decisions.

A creditor may ask your age, but if you're old enough to sign a binding contract (usually 18 or 21 years old depending on state law), a creditor may not:

- Turn you down or offer you less credit just because of your age; Ignore your retirement income in rating your application;
- Close your credit account or require you to reapply for it just because you reach a certain age or retire; or Deny you credit or close your account because credit life insurance or other credit-related insurance is not available to persons your age.

Creditors may "score" your age in a credit scoring system, but: if you are 62 or older you must be given at least as many points for age as any person under 62.

Because individuals' financial situations can change at different ages, the law lets creditors consider certain information related to age—such as how long until you retire or how long your income will continue. An older applicant might not qualify for a large loan with a 5 percent down payment on a risky venture, but might qualify for a smaller loan—with a bigger down payment—secured by good collateral.

> ***Remember that while declining income may be a handicap if you are older, you can usually offer a solid credit history to your advantage.***

The creditor has to look at all the facts and apply the usual standards of creditworthiness to your particular situation.

Public Assistance. Lenders cannot deny credit simply because you receive Social Security, disability benefits, or public assistance. However, they can assess whether this income is stable and will continue. But—as is the case with age—certain information related to this source of income could clearly affect creditworthiness. So, a creditor may consider such things as:

- how old your dependents are (because you may lose benefits when they reach a certain age); or
- whether you will continue to meet the residency requirements for receiving benefits.

This information helps the creditor determine the likelihood that your public assistance income will continue.

Housing Loans. The Equal Credit Opportunity Act covers your application for a mortgage or home improvement loan. It bans discrimination because of such characteristics as your race, color, gender, or because of the race or national origin of the people in the neighborhood where you live or want to buy your home. Nor may creditors use any appraisal of the value of the property that considers the race of the people in the neighborhood.

In addition, you are entitled to receive a copy of an appraisal report that you paid for in connection with an application for credit, if a you make a written request for the report.

DISCRIMINATION AGAINST WOMEN

Both men and women are protected from discrimination based on gender or marital status. But many of the law's provisions were designed to stop particular abuses that generally made if difficult for women to get credit. For example, the idea that single women ignore their debts when they marry, or that a woman's income "doesn't count" because she'll leave work to have children, now is unlawful in credit transactions.

The general rule is that you may not be denied credit just because you are a woman, or just because you are married, single, widowed, divorced, or separated. Here are some important protections:

Gender and Marital Status

Usually, creditors may not ask your gender on an application form (one exception is on a loan to buy or build a home).

You do not have to use Miss, Mrs., or Ms. with your name on a credit application. But, in some cases, a creditor may ask whether you are married, unmarried, or separated (unmarried includes single, divorced, and widowed).

Child-bearing Plans

Creditors may not ask about your birth control practices or whether you plan to have children, and they may not assume anything about those plans.

Income and Alimony

The creditor must count all of your income, even income from part- time employment.

Child support and alimony payments are a primary source of income for many women. You don't have to disclose these kinds of income, but if you do creditors must count them.

Communication and Contact Information

Lenders cannot deny credit based on whether you have a landline or personal phone listing. However, they may ask for a reliable way to contact you, including a mobile number or email address.

Your Own Accounts

In the past, women often needed a male cosigner to obtain credit. Today, the ECOA guarantees that all applicants—regardless of gender—can qualify for credit based on their individual income, assets, and credit history. Single women couldn't get loans because they were thought to be somehow less reliable than other applicants. You now have a fight to your own credit, based on your own credit records and earnings. Your own credit means a separate account or loan in your own name—not a joint account with your husband or a duplicate card on his account. Here are the rules:

- Creditors may not refuse to open an account just because of your gender or marital status. You can choose to use your first name and maiden name (Mary Smith); your first name and husband's last name (Mary Jones); or a combined last name (Mary Smith-Jones).
- If you're creditworthy, a creditor may not ask your husband to cosign your account, with certain exceptions when property rights are involved.
- Creditors may not ask for information about your husband or ex-husband when you apply for your own credit based on your own income—unless that income is alimony, child support, or separate maintenance payments from your spouse or former spouse.

This last rule, of course, does not apply if your husband is going to use your account or be responsible for paying your debts on the account, or if you live in a community property state. (Community property states are: Arizona, California, Idaho, Louisiana, Nevada, New Mexico, Texas, Washington and Wisconsin.)

Change in Marital Status

Married women have sometimes faced severe hardships when cut off from credit after their husbands died. Single women have had accounts closed when they married, and married women have had accounts closed after a divorce. The law says that creditors may not make you reapply for credit just because you marry or become widowed or divorced. Nor may they close your account or change the terms of your account on these grounds. There must be some sign that your creditworthiness has changed. For example, creditors may ask you to reapply if you relied on your ex-husband's income to get credit in the first place.

Setting up your own account protects you by giving you your own history of how you handle debt, to rely on if your financial situation changes because you are widowed or divorced. If you're getting married and plan to take your husband's surname, write to your creditors and tell them if you want to keep a separate account.

IF YOU'RE TURNED DOWN

Remember, your gender or race may not be used to discourage you from applying for a loan. And creditors may not hold up or otherwise delay your application on those grounds. Lenders must provide written notice within 30 days of a completed application, stating whether it was approved or denied. If denied, they must explain the reason or inform you of your right to request an explanation.If credit is denied, this notice must be in writing and it must explain the specific reasons why you were denied credit or tell you of your right to ask for an explanation. You have the same rights if an account you have had is closed.

If you are denied credit, be sure to find out why. Remember, you may have to ask the creditors for this explanation. It may be that the creditor thinks you have requested more money than you can repay on your income. It may be that you have not been employed or lived long enough in the community. You can discuss terms with the creditor and ways to improve your creditworthiness. The next chapter explains how to improve your ability to get credit.

If you think you have been discriminated against, cite the law to the lender. If the lender still says no without a satisfactory explanation, you may contact a Federal enforcement agency for assistance or bring legal action as described in the last chapter of this handbook.

DIGITAL LENDING AND ALTERNATIVE CREDIT SCORING

With the rise of online lending and fintech, some lenders now use alternative credit data—such as rent payments, utility bills, and even subscription services—to evaluate creditworthiness. If you have limited credit history, exploring these options may help you access credit.

11

CREDIT HISTORIES AND RECORDS

BUILDING UP A GOOD RECORD

Building your first credit history can be frustrating—it often feels like you need credit to qualify for credit. Some creditors will look only at your salary and job and the other financial information you put on your application. But most also want to know about your track record in handling credit—how reliably you've repaid past debts. They turn to the records kept by credit bureaus or credit reporting agencies whose business is to collect and store information about borrowers that is routinely supplied by many lenders. These records track your credit accounts, payment history, outstanding balances, and any missed or late payments.

Here are several ways you can begin to build up a good credit history:

- ❒ **Open a checking account or a savings account, or both.** These do not begin your credit file, but may be checked as evidence that you have money and know how to manage it. Cancelled checks can be used to show you pay utility bills or rent regularly, a sign of reliability.
- ❒ **Apply for a secured credit card or a department store credit card, which often have lower approval requirements.** Repaying credit card bills on time is a plus in credit histories. Consider secured credit cards, which require a refundable deposit as collateral and help establish credit with responsible use.
- ❒ **If you're new in town, write for a summary of any**

credit record kept by a credit bureau in your former town. Ask the bank or department store in your old hometown for the name of the agency it reports to.

If you don't qualify on the basis of your own credit standing, offer to have someone cosign your application. If you're turned down, find out why and try to clear up any misunderstandings.

WHAT LAWS APPLY?

The following laws can help you start your credit history and keep your record accurate:

- The **Equal Credit Opportunity Act** gives women a way to start their own credit history and identity.
- The **Fair Credit Reporting Act** sets up a procedure for correcting mistakes on your credit record.

CREDIT HISTORIES FOR WOMEN

Under the Equal Credit Opportunity Act, reports to credit bureaus must be made in the names of both husband and wife if both use an account or are responsible for repaying the debt. Historically, many women faced challenges building independent credit histories because accounts were often listed solely under their husband's name. Today, credit laws ensure that past joint accounts contribute to both spouses' credit profiles But they can still benefit from this record.

Under the Equal Credit Opportunity Act, creditors must consider the credit history of accounts women have held jointly with their husbands. Creditors must also look at the record of any account held only in the husband's name if a woman can show it also reflects her own creditworthiness. If the record is unfavorable—if an ex-husband was a bad credit risk—she can try to show that the record does not reflect her own reputation. Remember that a wife may also open her own account to be sure of starting her own credit history.

Here's an example:

> *Mary Jones, when married to John Jones, always paid their credit card bills on time and from their joint checking account. But the card was issued in John's name, and the credit bureau kept all records in John's name. Now Mary is a widow and wants to take out a new card, but she's told she has no credit history. To benefit from the good credit record already on the books in John's name, Mary should point out that she handled all accounts properly when she was married and that bills were paid by checks from their joint checking account.*

MAINTAINING AN ACCURATE CREDIT REPORT"

Mistakes on your credit record—sometimes mistaken identities—can cloud your credit future. Your credit rating is important, so be sure credit bureau records are complete and accurate.

The Fair Credit Reporting Act says that you must be told what's in your credit file and have any errors corrected.

Handling Negative Marks on Your Credit Report

If a lender denies your credit application due to negative information in your credit report, they must provide you with the name and contact details of the credit bureau that supplied the report. Then, you may either request information from the credit bureau by mail or in person.

You will not get an exact copy of the file, but you will at least learn what's in the report. The law also says that the credit bureau must help you interpret the data—because it's raw data that takes experience to analyze. If you're questioning a credit refusal made within the past 30 days, the bureau is not allowed to charge a fee for giving you information.

Any error that you find must be investigated by the credit bureau with the creditor who supplied the data. The bureau will remove from your credit file any errors the creditor admits are there. If you disagree with the findings, you can file a short statement in your record giving your side of the story. Future reports to creditors must include this statement or a summary of it.

Old Information

Sometimes credit information is too old to give a good picture of your financial reputation. There is a limit on how long certain kinds of information may be kept in your file:

Bankruptcies must be taken off your credit history after 10 years. Suits and judgments, tax liens, arrest records, and most other kinds of unfavorable information must be dropped after 7 years.

Your credit record may not be given to anyone who does not have a legitimate business need for it. Stores to which you are applying for credit or prospective employers may examine your record; curious neighbors may not.

Correcting Billing Errors and Disputes

In the next chapter, you will find the steps to take if there's an error on your bill. By following these steps, you can protect your credit rating.

"DIGITAL CREDIT-BUILDING SOLUTIONS"

Today, alternative credit-building options exist beyond traditional credit cards and loans. Some fintech companies report rent, utility, and subscription payments to credit bureaus, helping individuals establish or improve credit without taking on new debt.

Services like Experian Boost, eCredable, and UltraFICO use alternative data such as banking history to improve credit scores. Buy Now, Pay Later (BNPL) services like Affirm and Klarna can impact credit scores depending on reporting practices.

12

OTHER ASPECTS OF USING CREDIT

The best way to keep up your credit standing is to repay all debts on time. But there may be complications. To protect your credit rating, you should learn how to correct mistakes and misunderstandings that can tangle up your credit accounts.

When there's a snag, first try to deal directly with the creditor. The credit laws can help you settle your complaints without a hassle.

WHAT LAWS APPLY?

Fair Credit Billing Act sets up procedures requiring creditors to promptly correct billing mistakes; allowing you to withhold payments on defective goods; and requiring creditors to promptly credit your payments.

Truth In Lending gives you three days to change your mind about certain credit transactions that use your home as collateral; it also limits your risk on lost or stolen credit cards.

BILLING ERRORS

Month after month John Jones was billed for a lawn mower he never ordered and never got. Finally, he tore up his bill and mailed back the pieces—just to try to explain things to a person instead of a computer.

There's a more effective, easier way to straighten out these errors. The Fair Credit Billing Act requires creditors to correct errors promptly and without damage to your credit rating.

A Case of Error

The law defines a billing error as any charge: for something you didn't buy or for a purchase made by someone not authorized to use your account; that is not properly identified on your bill or is for an amount different from the actual purchase price or was entered on a date different from the purchase date; or for something that you did not accept on delivery or that was not delivered according to agreement.

Billing errors also include:

- errors in arithmetic;
- failure to show a payment or other credit to your account;
- failure to mail the bill to your current address, if you told the
- creditor about an address change at least 20 days before the end of the billing period;
- a questionable item, or an item for which you need more information.

In Case of Error

If you think your bill is wrong, or want more information about it, follow these steps:

❒ **Notify the creditor in writing within 60 days after the first bill was mailed that showed the error.** Be sure to write to the address the creditor lists for billing inquiries and to tell the creditor: your name and account number; that you believe the bill contains an error and why you believe it is wrong; and the date and suspected amount of the error or the item you want explained.

❒ **Pay all parts of the bill that are not in dispute.** But, while waiting for an answer, you do not have to pay the amount in question (the "disputed amount") or any minimum payments or finance charges that apply to it.

- ❐ **The creditor must acknowledge your letter within 30 days, unless the problem can be resolved within that time.** Within two billing periods—but in no case longer than 90 days—either your account must be corrected or you must be told why the creditor believes the bill is correct.
- ❐ **If the creditor made a mistake, you do not pay any finance charges on the disputed amount.** Your account must be corrected, and you must be sent an explanation of any amount you still owe.
- ❐ **If no error is found, the creditor must send you an explanation of the reasons for that finding and promptly send a statement of what you owe, which may include any finance charges that have accumulated and any minimum payments you missed while you were questioning the bill.** You then have the time usually given on your type of account to pay any balance, but not less that 10 days.
- ❐ **If you still are not satisfied, you should notify the creditor in writing within the time allowed to pay your bill.**

MAINTAINING YOUR CREDIT RATING

A creditor may not threaten your credit rating while you're resolving a billing dispute.

Once you have written about a possible error, a creditor must not give out information to other creditors or credit bureaus that would hurt your credit reputation. And, until your complaint is answered, the creditor also may not take any action to collect the disputed amount.

After the creditor has explained the bill, if you do not pay in the time allowed, you may be reported as delinquent on the amount in dispute and the creditor may take action to collect. Even so, you can still disagree in writing. Then the creditor must report that you have challenged your bill and give you the name and address of each person who has received information about your account. When the matter is settled, the creditor must report the outcome to each person who has received information. Remember that you may also place your own side of the story in your credit record.

DEFECTIVE GOODS OR SERVICES

Your new sofa arrives with only three legs. You try to return it; no luck. You ask the merchant to repair or replace it; still no luck. The Fair Credit Billing Act allows you to withhold payment on any damaged or poor quality goods or services purchased with a credit card, as long as you have made a real attempt to solve the problem with the merchant.

This right may be limited if the card was a bank or travel and entertainment card or any card not issued by the store where you made your purchase. In such cases, the sale: must have been for more than $50; and must have taken place in your home state or within 100 miles of your home address.

PROMPT CREDIT FOR PAYMENTS AND REFUNDS FOR CREDIT BALANCES

Many creditors offer a grace period, allowing you to avoid interest if you pay your balance within a certain timeframe. This makes timely billing and payment processing essential. With online banking and auto-pay options, it's easier than ever to manage payments efficiently. Always verify your statements to ensure your payments are credited accurately. Check your statements to make sure your creditor follows these rules:

- **Billing.** Look at the date on the postmark. If your account is one on which no finance or other charge is added before a certain due date, then creditors must mail their statements at least 14 days before payment is due.

- **Crediting.** Look at the payment date entered on the statement. Creditors must credit payments on the day they arrive, as long as you pay according to payment instructions. This means, for example, sending your payment to the address listed on the bill.
- **Credit Balances.** If a credit balance results on your account (for example, because you pay more than the amount you owe, or you return a purchase and the purchase price is credited to your account), the creditor must make a refund to you. The refund must be made within seven business days after your written request, or automatically if the credit balance is still in existence after six months.

CANCELLING A MORTGAGE

Truth in Lending gives you a chance to change your mind on one important kind of transaction—when you use your home as security for a credit transaction. For example, when you are financing a major repair or remodeling and use your home as security, you have three business days, usually after you sign a contract, to think about the transaction and to cancel it if you wish. The creditor must give you written notice of your right to cancel, and, if you decide to cancel, you must notify the creditor in writing within the three-day period. The creditor must then return all fees paid and cancel the security interest in your home. No contractor may start work on your home, and no lender may pay you or the contractor until the three days are up. If you must have the credit immediately to meet a financial emergency, you may give up your right to cancel by providing a written explanation of the circumstances.

The right to cancel (or right of rescission) was provided to protect you against hasty decisions—or decisions made under pressure—that might put your home at risk if you are unable to repay the loan. The law does not apply to a mortgage to finance the purchase of your home; for that, you commit yourself as soon as you sign the mortgage contract. And, if you use your home to secure an open-end credit line—a home equity line, for instance—you have the right the cancel when you open the account or when your security interest or credit limit is increased. (In the case of an increase, only the increase would be cancelled.)

LOST OR STOLEN CREDIT CARDS

If your wallet is stolen, your greatest cost may be inconvenience, because your liability on lost or stolen cards is limited under Truth in Lending.

You do not have to pay for any unauthorized charges made after you notify the card company of loss or theft of your card. So keep a list of your credit card numbers and notify card issuers immediately if your card is lost or stolen. The most you will have to pay for unauthorized charges is $50 on each card—even if someone runs up several hundred dollars worth of charges before you report a card missing.

UNSOLICITED CARDS

It is illegal for card issuers to send you a credit card unless you ask for or agree to receive one. However, a card issuer may send, without your request, a new card to replace an expiring one.

ELECTRONIC FUND TRANSFERS—INSTANT MONEY

On his way home last Friday night, John Jones realized he had no cash for the weekend. The bank was closed, but John had his bank debit card and the code to use it. He inserted the card into an automated teller machine outside the front door of the bank; then, using a number keyboard, he entered his code and pressed the buttons for a withdrawal of $50. John's cash was dispensed automatically from the machine, and his bank account was electronically debited for the $50 cash withdrawal.

John's debit card is just one of many ways to use electronic fund transfer (EFT) systems, which now include digital wallets like Apple Pay, Google Pay, and peer-to-peer payment apps such as Venmo and Zelle. These systems enable instant, paperless transactions.

EFT in Operation

The national payment mechanism moves money between accounts in a fast, paperless way. These are some examples of EFT systems in operation:

- **Teller Machines (ATMs).** Consumers can do their banking without the assistance of a teller, as john Jones did to get cash, or to make deposits, pay bills, or transfer funds from one account to another electronically. These machines are used with a debit or EFT card and a code, which is often called a personal identification number or "PIN."
- **(POS) Transactions.** Some EFT cards can be used when shopping to allow the transfer of funds from the consumer's account to the merchant's. To pay for a purchase, the consumer presents an EFT card instead of a check or cash. Money is taken out of the consumer's account and put into the merchant's account electronically.
- **Preauthorized Transfers.** This is a method of automatically depositing to or withdrawing funds from an individual's account, when the account holder authorizes the bank or a third party (such as an employer) to do so. For example, consumers can authorize direct electronic deposit of wages, Social Security or dividend payments to their accounts. Or, they can authorize financial institutions to make regular,

ongoing payments of insurance, mortgage, utility or other bills.

- **Telephone Transfers.** Consumers can transfer funds from one account to another—from savings to checking, for example—or can order payment of specific bills by phone.

What Law Applies?

The **Electronic Funds Transfer Act** gives consumers answers to several basic questions about using EFT services.

A check is a piece of paper with information that authorizes a bank to withdraw a certain amount of money from one person's account and pay that amount to another person. Most consumer questions center on the fact that EFT systems transmit the information without the paper. Thus, they ask:

- What record—what evidence—will I have of my transactions? How easily will I be able to correct errors?
- What if someone steals money from my account? What about solicitations?
- Do I have to use EFT services?

Here are the answers the EFT Act gives to consumer questions about these systems.

What Record Will I Have of My Transactions?

A cancelled check is permanent proof that a payment has been made. Is proof of payment available with EFT services?

The answer is yes. When using an ATM, point-of-sale terminal, or mobile payment app, you receive a digital or printed receipt showing the amount, date, and transaction details. Many banks now provide real-time alerts via email or text, helping consumers track spending instantly. This receipt is your record of transfers initiated at an electronic terminal.

Your digital or paper bank statement includes a full record of electronic transactions, whether via debit card, automated transfers, mobile banking apps, or direct deposits. Many banks also offer budgeting tools that categorize these transactions for easier tracking. It will also name the party to whom payment has been made and show any fees for EFT services (or the total amount charged for account maintenance) and your opening and closing balances.

Your monthly statement is proof of payment to another person, your record for tax or other purposes, and your way of checking and reconciling EFT transactions with your bank balance.

How Easily Will I Be Able to Correct Errors?

The way to report errors is somewhat different with EFT services than it is with credit cards. But, as with credit cards, financial institutions must investigate and correct promptly any EFT errors you report.

If you believe there has been an error in an electronic fund transfer relating to your account:

- ❒ **Write or call your financial institution immediately if possible, but no later than 60 days from the date the first statement that you think shows an error was mailed to you.** Give your name and account number and explain why you believe there is an error, what kind of error, and the dollar amount and date in question. If you call, you may be asked to send this information in writing within 10 business days.

- ❒ **The financial institution must promptly investigate an error and resolve it within 45 days.** However, if the financial institution takes longer than 10 business days to complete its investigation, generally it must put back into your account the amount in question while it finishes the investigation. (The time periods are longer for POS debit card transactions and for any EFT transaction initiated outside the United States.) In the meantime, you will have full use of the funds in question.

- ❒ **The financial institution must notify you of the results of its investigation.** If there was an error, the institution must correct it promptly—for example, by making a recredit final.
- ❒ **If it finds no error, the financial institution must explain in writing why it believes no error occurred and let you know that it has deducted any amount recredited during the investigation.** You may ask for copies of documents relied on in the investigation.

What About Loss or Theft?

It's important to be aware of the potential risk in using an EFT card, which differs from the risk on a credit card.

On lost or stolen credit cards, your loss is limited to $50 per card. On an EFT card, your liability for an unauthorized withdrawal can vary.

Your loss is limited to $50 if you notify the financial institution within two business days after learning of loss or theft of your card or code.

But, you could lose as much as $500 if you do not tell the card issuer within two business days after learning of the loss or theft.

If you do not report an unauthorized transfer that appears on your statement within 60 days after the statement is mailed to you, you risk unlimited loss on transfers made after the 60-day period. That means you could lose all the money in your account plus your maximum overdraft line of credit.

Example: On Monday, john's debit card and secret code were stolen. On Tuesday, the thief withdrew $250, all the money John had in his checking account. Five days later, the thief withdrew another $500, triggering John's overdraft line of credit. John did not realize his card was stolen until he received a statement from the bank, showing withdrawals of $750 he did not make. He called the bank right away. John's liability is $50.

Now suppose that when john got his bank statement he didn't look at it and didn't call the bank. Seventy days after the statement was mailed to john, the thief withdrew another $1,000, reaching the limit on John's line of credit. In this case, John would be liable for $1,050 ($50 for transfers before the end of the 60 days; $1,000 for transfers made more than 60 days after the statement was mailed).

What About Solicitations?

A financial institution may send you an EFT card that is VALID FOR USE only if you ask for one, or to replace or renew an expiring card. The financial institution must also give you the following information about your rights and responsibilities:

- A notice of your liability in case the card is lost or stolen;
- A telephone number for reporting loss or theft of the card or an unauthorized transfer;
- A description of its error resolution procedures;
- The kinds of electronic fund transfers you may make and any limits on the frequency or dollar amounts of such transfers;
- Any charge by the institution for using EFT services; Your right to receive records of electronic fund transfers; How to stop payment of a preauthorized transfer;
- The financial institution's liability to you for any failure to make or to stop transfers; and

- The conditions under which a financial institution will give information to third parties about your account.

Generally, you must also get advance notice of any change in the account that would increase your costs or liability, or limit transfers.

A financial institution may send you a card you did not request only if the card is NOT VALID FOR USE. An "unsolicited" card can be validated only at your request and only after the institution makes sure that you are the person whose name is on the card. It must also be sent with instructions on how to dispose of an unwanted card.

Do I Have to Use EFT?

The EFT Act forbids a creditor from requiring you to repay a loan or other credit by EFT, except in the case of overdraft checking plans. And, although your employer or a government agency can require you to receive your salary or a government benefit by electronic transfer, you have the right to choose the financial institution that will receive your funds.

SPECIAL QUESTIONS ABOUT PREAUTHORIZED PLANS

Q. How will I know a preauthorized credit has been made?

A. There are various ways you may be notified. Notice may be given by your employer (or whoever is sending the funds) that the deposit has been sent to your financial institution. Otherwise, a financial institution may provide notice when it has received the credit or will send you a notice only when it has not received the funds. Financial institutions also have the option of giving you a telephone number you can call to check on a preauthorized credit.

Q. How do I stop a preauthorized payment?

A. You may stop any preauthorized payment by calling or writing the financial institution, so that your order is received at least three business days before the payment date. Written confirmation of a telephone notice to stop payment may be required.

Q. If the payments I preauthorize vary in amount from month to month, how will I know how much will be transferred out of my account?

A. You have the right to be notified of all varying payments at least 10 days in advance.

Or, you may choose to specify a range of amounts and to be told only when a transfer falls outside that range. You may also choose to be told only when a transfer differs by a certain amount from the previous payment to the same company.

Q. Do the EFT Act protections apply to all preauthorized plans?

A. No. They do not apply to automatic transfers from your account to the institution that holds your account or vice versa. For example, they do not apply to automatic payments made on a mortgage held by the financial institution where you have your EFT account. The EFT Act also does not apply to automatic transfers among your accounts at one financial institution.

The rise of fintech has transformed electronic payments. Consumers now use mobile wallets, peer-to-peer payment apps, and AI-powered budgeting tools to manage finances effortlessly. As EFTs evolve, it's important to stay aware of security measures, such as multi-factor authentication and fraud monitoring, to protect your accounts.

13

COMPLAINING ABOUT CREDIT

COMPLAINING TO FEDERAL ENFORCEMENT AGENCIES

Start by addressing your issue directly with the creditor, as most problems can be resolved through communication. If that doesn't work, you can escalate your complaint using the formal processes outlined in this chapter. Here's the way to file a complaint with the Federal agencies responsible for carrying out consumer credit protection laws.

Complaints About Banks

If you have a complaint about a bank in connection with any of the Federal credit laws—or if you think any part of your business with a bank has been handled in an unfair or deceptive way—you may get advice and help from the Federal Reserve. The practice you complain about does not have to be covered by Federal law. Furthermore, you don't have to be a customer of the bank to file a complaint.

If your complaint involves a bank or financial institution, you can submit it to the appropriate regulatory agency. **The Federal Reserve's Division of Consumer and Community Affairs** accepts complaints regarding state-chartered banks that are members of the Federal Reserve System. You can also file a complaint online through the **Consumer Financial Protection Bureau (CFPB)** at *www.consumerfinance.gov*. Be sure to describe the bank practice you are complaining about and give the name and address of the bank involved.

The Federal Reserve will write back within 15 days—sometimes with an answer, sometimes telling you that more time is needed to handle your complaint. The additional time is required when complex issues are involved or when the complaint will be investigated by a Federal Reserve Bank. When this is the case, the Federal Reserve will try to keep you informed about the progress being made.

Different agencies oversee different financial institutions. If the Federal Reserve does not regulate your bank, it will direct your complaint to the appropriate agency. You can also check the CFPB's website to find the correct agency to contact.

Complaints About Other Institutions

Many financial regulators do not handle individual disputes, but they use consumer complaints to track trends and enforce laws. If your issue is not resolved through direct action, submitting a complaint can still help improve industry practices.

PENALTIES UNDER THE LAWS

You may also take legal action against a creditor. If you decide to bring a lawsuit, here are the penalties a creditor must pay if you win.

Truth in Lending and Consumer Leasing Acts

If a creditor fails to provide required disclosures, gives inaccurate information, or violates the rules governing credit cards and home-secured loans, you may sue for actual damages. This includes financial losses due to misrepresentation. Additionally, for certain violations, you may recover statutory damages, which can range from $100 to $1,000, depending on the circumstances.

In addition, you can sue for twice the finance charge in the case of certain credit disclosures, or, if a lease is concerned, 25 percent of total monthly payments. In either case, the least the court may award you if you win is $100, and the most is $1,000. In any lawsuit that you win, you are entitled to reimbursement for court costs and attorney's fees.

Class action suits are also permitted. A class action suit is one filed on behalf of a group of people with similar claims.

Equal Credit Opportunity Act

If you think you can prove that a creditor has discriminated against you for any reason prohibited by the Act, you as an individual may sue for actual damages plus punitive damages—that is, damages for the fact that the law has been violated—of up to $10,000. In a successful lawsuit, the court will award you court costs and a reasonable amount for attorney's fees. Class action suits are also permitted.

Fair Credit Billing Act

A creditor who breaks the rules for the correction of billing errors automatically loses the amount owed on the item in question and any finance charges on it, up to a combined total of $50—even if the bill was correct. You as an individual may also sue for actual damages plus twice the amount of any finance charges, but in any case not less than $100 nor more than $1,000. You are also entitled to court costs and attorney's fees in a successful lawsuit. Class action suits are also permitted.

Fair Credit Reporting Act

You may sue any credit reporting agency or creditor for breaking the rules about who may see your credit records or for not correcting errors in your file. Again, you are entitled to actual damages, plus punitive damages that the court may allow if the violation is proved to have been intentional. In any successful lawsuit, you will also be awarded court costs and attorney's fees. A person who obtains a credit report without proper authorization—or an employee of a credit reporting agency who gives a credit report to unauthorized persons—may be fined up to $5,000 or imprisoned for one year, or both.

Electronic Fund Transfer Act

If a financial institution does not follow the provisions of the EFT Act, you may sue for actual damages (or in certain cases when the institution fails to correct an error or recredit an account, for three times actual damages) plus punitive damages of not less than $100 nor more than $1,000. You are also entitled to court costs and attorney's fees in a successful lawsuit. Class action suits are also permitted.

If an institution fails to make an electronic fund transfer, or to stop payment of a preauthorized transfer when properly instructed by you to do so, you may sue for all damages that result from the failure.

CONSUMER COMPLAINT RESOURCES

Today, consumers have additional options for resolving credit disputes:

- ❒ **Consumer Financial Protection Bureau (CFPB).** File complaints online at *www.consumerfinance.gov* for issues related to credit cards, loans, and financial institutions.
- ❒ **Federal Trade Commission (FTC).** Report fraudulent credit practices at *www.ftc.gov.*
- ❒ **Online Reviews & Social Media.** Public complaints on platforms like the Better Business Bureau (BBB) or Trustpilot can prompt businesses to respond more quickly.
- ❒ **State Attorneys General: Many state consumer protection offices provide legal assistance for credit disputes.**

14

YOUR ROADMAP TO FINANCIAL FREEDOM

BRINGING IT ALL TOGETHER

By now, you have gained an extensive understanding of credit—how it works, how to improve it, how to use it wisely, and how to protect it. Whether you are looking to rebuild your credit, establish a strong financial foundation, or leverage credit for business and real estate ventures, the strategies in this book are your blueprint to success.

Credit is a powerful tool, but like any tool, it must be used with knowledge and care. Good credit can open doors to opportunities, while poor credit can create roadblocks. The good news is that credit is not static—your financial habits and decisions today can improve your credit and shape your financial future.

Your goal should be to master credit and use it to build wealth, not debt. Too many people let credit control them. Those who succeed use credit as a stepping stone to bigger financial opportunities. This is how businesses grow, fortunes are made, and financial security is built.

YOUR CREDIT SUCCESS CHECKLIST

Use this checklist as your step-by-step guide to taking control of your credit:

Step 1: Assess Your Current Credit Situation

- Request your free credit reports from all three major credit bureaus—Experian, Equifax, and TransUnion—at *www.annualcreditreport.com*. Due to federal law changes, you can now check your reports weekly for free.

- Check your credit score through reputable services like FICO, Experian, or Credit Karma to understand your financial standing.
- Identify and dispute any inaccurate, outdated, or fraudulent items on your credit report.

Step 2: Strengthen Your Credit Profile

- Pay all bills on time—set up automatic payments if needed.
- Keep credit card balances low (below 30% of your available credit limit).
- Avoid applying for multiple credit accounts in a short time period.
- Mix up your credit—having a combination of installment loans and revolving credit can help.
- Keep older credit accounts open to maintain a longer credit history.
- Avoid carrying high balances on multiple cards; lenders look at overall credit utilization.

Step 3: Rebuilding Credit After Financial Struggles

- Use secured credit cards, credit-builder loans, or rent-reporting services to start improving your credit score.
- Become an authorized user on a responsible person's credit account to build positive payment history.
- If you're struggling with debt, explore hardship programs, debt repayment plans, or credit counseling services.
- Use a co-signer or authorized user strategy to rebuild credit.
- Make consistent, on-time payments on all financial obligations.
- Gradually increase credit limits over time while maintaining low utilization.

- Be proactive about negotiating with creditors if you are struggling to make payments. Many will offer hardship programs or lower interest rates if you ask.

Step 4: Using Credit Wisely for Business and Investments

- Use business credit cards and lines of credit to separate personal and business expenses—this helps build business credit while protecting your personal finances.
- Consider SBA loans, microloans, or alternative financing for business expansion instead of relying solely on personal credit.
- Real estate investors should explore commercial loans, DSCR (Debt Service Coverage Ratio) loans, and other credit-based financing options to scale their portfolios responsibly.
- Never use personal credit for business expenses unless absolutely necessary. Keeping finances separate is critical for long-term financial growth.

Step 5: Protecting Your Credit and Avoiding Pitfalls

- Set up fraud alerts or credit freezes if you suspect identity theft.
- Monitor your credit regularly using services like Credit Karma or Experian.
- Beware of predatory lenders, payday loans, and high-interest borrowing.
- Stay informed about changing credit laws and regulations.
- Never co-sign a loan unless you are willing to take full responsibility for the debt.

THE POWER IS IN YOUR HANDS

Your financial future is shaped by the credit decisions you make today. Improving and maintaining strong credit requires consistency and smart decision-making, but the rewards are long-lasting. Credit is more than just a financial score—it's a gateway to opportunities, from homeownership to entrepreneurship and investment growth. It is a journey rather than an overnight fix. However, by following the principles outlined in this book, you can set yourself up for long-term financial success.

- **Credit is a tool, not free money. Use it strategically.**
- **Your credit score is a reflection of your financial habits—make them good ones.**
- **Even if you've made mistakes in the past, you can always rebuild.**

Some of the most successful businesspeople in the world got where they are today by mastering credit. They didn't just use credit—they leveraged it. They turned borrowed money into profits, used credit to scale their businesses, and ensured that they had access to capital when opportunity knocked. You can do the same.

THE NEXT STEPS TO FINANCIAL INDEPENDENCE

- ❒ **Automate your credit management.** Set up automatic payments and use budgeting apps like Mint or YNAB.
- ❒ **Expand your financial literacy.** Follow industry experts, read investment and finance books, and stay updated on credit laws.
- ❒ **Strategize your next major credit move.** Whether it's buying a home, securing business funding, or leveraging credit for investments.
- ❒ **Commit to long-term credit success.** Good credit

isn't just about fixing past mistakes; it's about creating a financially secure future.

The best time to start improving your credit is today. Begin with one step at a time, stay consistent, and before you know it, you'll have a strong financial foundation that supports your goals and dreams.

Now, take action—your financial future is waiting!

15

POWER CREDIT METHODS FOR SMALL BUSINESS OWNERS AND ENTREPRENEURS

USE SUBPRIME MORTGAGE FOR WEAK BORROWING CREDIT

People who want to buy income real estate sometimes have poor credit. They call and ask: "Can I still get into income real estate with poor credit?" Or: "I have no credit at all. Can I borrow?"

The good news is that, yes, you can still qualify for financing—even with weak or no credit—by using a subprime mortgage. However, the availability of these loans fluctuates based on economic conditions. During financial downturns, lenders may restrict subprime mortgage offerings, making them harder to obtain. For example, at the time of this writing, the subprime mortgage industry has been in poor shape for a year or more, which means it may be harder to get a subprime mortgage loan at this time.

In general, with a subprime mortgage you pay a higher interest rate than a conventional mortgage since risk is greater. Your goal is to get the income real estate that will give you the monthly income that can free you from a routine job and threats of layoffs. Remembering that the higher interest you pay is both provable and tax-deductible as a business expense.

Where can I find subprime lenders and what should I watch out for?"

Here are your answers. Subprime lenders:

- Advertise in local papers with headlines or ad copy saying: "Bad credit OK;" Or: "No credit check;" Or: "Bankruptcy OK;" Or: "No income check."
- Offer home equity loans saying: "100% equity loans; Or: "125% equity loans;" Or "Pay off all your bills using the equity in your home;" Or: "Pay $—- per month for 15 years-get $100,000 tomorrow."
- If you can't find such lenders in your area, look in nearby large-city newspapers and Yellow Pages for such lenders. Call and ask them to recommend a lender in your area.. They'll be happy to do so fox you.

And what should I look out for?

Here are a some items you should check BEFORE signing papers for a subprime mortgage:

- **Avoid excessive interest rates.** The rate charged for a subprirne mortgage should not be more than 8% above comparable Treasury securities. If there are "points" charged for the loan, the number of points should be added to the interest rate to find the total of 8%, or less.

- **Watch out for excessive fees which the lender may try to charge for the subprime mortgage.** Use your head and decide if a proposed fee is excessive by estimating how much work has to be done on the loan. Thus, a fee of $10,000 on a $100,000 loan (10%) is too high. Wheel and deal to have the fee reduced to 5% or less.

HOW TO GET LOANS WHEN YOUR CREDIT IS BAD

We're often asked: "How can I get a real estate (or business) loan when my credit is bad?" Or "When I have no credit at all?"

The answer is:

Bring in a partner who has GOOD credit and allow your partner's credit to get you your loan.

You do all the work on the real estate or business and give your partner a portion of the ownership—called an "equity kicker" and a portion of any profit earned by the business.

Limiting the equity kicker to 5% of the value of the real estate or business and the profit sharing to 10%, or less, depending on what you can work out.

While you rebuild your credit or establish it for the first time using the income from real estate or business to get credit cards, a line of credit, etc.

How and Where Can I Get Partners?

The answer is: "You have to look for them."

"But where," you ask.

Here are your answers-some of which may work for you

- ❒ **Make a list of your relatives, friends, business associates and any other people who might want to work you your in your business deals.**
- ❒ **Rate them as Prime, Possible, Maybe, or None Candidates based on what you know about them.**
- ❒ **Prepare a spoken request that you'll make in person or by phone to your Prime, Possible and Maybe Candidates.** Speak it out loud to yourself and see how it sounds. Improve it as much as you can, removing words that don't sound right.
- ❒ **Call your candidates.** Speak your piece and see what sort of response you get. Don't be turned off by refusals. Just go to the next person. on the list.
- ❒ **Write a letter for distant Candidates and send, it to them.** You can base it on your spoken request.
- ❒ **Run ads in local papers, under the "Business Op-**

portunities" heading saying: "PARTNER NEEDED for lucrative business. Call 123-4567."

- ❒ **Find your partner.** Get your loan. Start, or buy, your business; get the credit you deserve; build your wealth in your own business!

HOW TO OVERCOME A POOR CREDIT RATING TO GET THE LOANS YOU NEED

A Poor credit rating can haunt a loan applicant. Many such people will say: "I've got great deals I can do in real estate or business but I can't get a loan because my credit rating is bad. What can I do?"

You can:

- ❒ **Work around poor credit by getting a cosigner for the loan you need.** Pay your cosigner a suitable fee for helping you get the loan by using their credit rating. NOTE: Your cosigner could be the real estate/business seller.
- ❒ **Have the seller of the real estate or business you're buying take out a loan in their name for the down payment on what you're buying.** You assume responsibility for repaying the loan out of the earnings of the real estate or business you're buying, using its income for payments.
- ❒ **Get a partner for your real estate or business firm.** Have your partner apply for any loan you need, with you acting as cosigner for your partner, who has good credit.
- ❒ **Form a corporation for your real estate or business deals.** Have the corporation apply for the business loan(s) you need. With some lenders your personal credit will not be questioned. Other lend-

ers may want you to cosign your corporation's loan application.

- ❒ **Buy into a "zero down" property using any of the Federal, State or City programs offering such financing for first-time home owners.** Some programs ignore the buyer's credit rating. Once you've owned the property for six months or so, apply for a home equity loan. As a home owner, your credit rating is less of a factor in getting any loan you seek.
- ❒ **Get a secured credit card (where you deposit anywhere from $300 to $500 in a bank account and your credit-card charges are secured by this interest-eaming cash.** Pay your credit card charge ahead of time. Soon—after 6 months to a year—you'll be offered an unsecured card. This puts you on the road to strong credit while doing your deals.
- ❒ **Advertise (free in ATTAIN: The IW$ Newsletter; see** *IWSNewsletter.com*) **for cosigners to make your loan application more acceptable to lenders.** You can also advertise in your local newspapers and magazines. Join the local apartment owners group or Chamber of Commerce and attend meetings to meet people who may have real estate or a business for sale. Becoming friendly with such people can lead to getting the real estate or business you want with no credit check. Result? You get the income you seek—without worrying about poor credit.

Start improving your credit now! You can overcome a poor credit rating and get the real estate or business you want? Just take the ideas above and use them—NOW!

GETTING YOUR LOAN EVEN AFTER GETTING TURNED DOWN

People ask again and again, "How can I got the loan I need for this great deal—after I've been turned down by three lenders?"

There's s no one answer to this question. But here are answers that do work:

- ❒ **Find out why you were turned down.** How do you do this? Just ask the lender: "Why was I turned down" 1 want to know the exact reason for the turn-down."
- ❒ **Ask the lender: "Who do you think might make this loan to me, in view of the turn-down?"** Many lenders know other lenders seeking to make loans. If the lender likes your presentation and the deal (Teal estate business) he/she might help you by naming a lender.
- ❒ **Probe further.** Ask "How can I improve my loan application to make it more acceptable to any lender?" Your lender may be willing to point out parts of your loan application that could be improved, increasing your chances of quick and happy loan approval. Often, a loan application will have a glaring error or on Fission that the applicant doesn't see but a lender does, And most lenders will be happy to show you.
- ❒ **Research lenders who make the type of loan you need.** Sometimes a borrower will apply at the first lender he/she runs across, without knowing the lender's preferences as to type of loan, size of loan, repayment time (called term), loan purpose, etc.
- ❒ **Pick lenders that make the type of loan you seek Thus choice is often half the victory.** Lenders want to make loans. They want to make loans they feel

comfortable and experienced with. If your loan suits the lender you apply to, your chances for quick, and happy, approval zoom!

- ❒ **Get the loan application for your new lender and have it typed throughout.** Make the app "gleam" in appearance because it is so neatly done. Such apps get a much higher rate of approval than sloppy, poorly prepared ones that shout carelessness to their viewers, the loan officer who approves (or disapproves) them!
- ❒ **Accept the lender's terms—-don't argue over interest .rate, duration (term) of the loan, repayment schedule, or other requirements your lender may set.** Your goal is to GET THE LOAN! You can always refinance at a later date on your terms. But for now, GET THE LOAN-it's your goal and what you want!

GET AN EASY, FLEXIBLE, "ANYTHING" LOAN

Have you tried an Anything Loan lately? You might be pleasantly surprised at how simple it is to get one. An Anything Loan—an unsecured, no-collateral personal loan—can provide up to $50,000 in cash, making it a welcome option for anyone looking for fast, flexible funding.

Why Anything Loans Are More Accessible Than Ever

The lending world has changed, and personal loans are more attractive than ever. More banks are offering them, and more lenders are expanding their reach. Thanks to digital banking, you're no longer limited to a handful of local lenders.

> *Tip: Apply to both local and national lenders to increase your chances of approval.*

Submitting a Loan Application Has Never Been Easier

Why? Two big reasons:

- Personal loan applications are some of the simplest to complete.
- You have more ways than ever to apply.

You can apply by phone, mail, fax, or online. Many banks even offer "Loans by Phone," while lenders proudly display current interest rates and easy-to-use loan calculators on their websites.

Time-Honored Features That Make Personal Loans a Great Choice

- **Use it for anything.** No restrictions, no red tape. Need cash for business? No problem. Unlike business loans, you're not tied to specific uses outlined in a loan agreement.
- **Save money in the long run.** Compared to a credit line, personal loans often come with lower interest rates, meaning you pay less over time.
- **Easier approval than business loans.** No business plan, no collateral, no need to put up your own cash first. Just apply and go.
- **Need more than one?** If one personal loan isn't enough, you can apply for another.

Three of the Sweetest Words Ever Uttered: "No Collateral Required"

This alone explains why the Anything Loan has been—and likely always will be—one of the most popular and straightforward loans around.

A Borrower's Best Friend

Even if the loan amount—typically $35,000 or less—seems modest, an Anything Loan is quick, simple, and incredibly useful. It can help you:

- Set up or expand a business
- Close a lucrative real estate deal
- Buy equipment or raw materials
- Take that much-needed vacation

An Anything Loan can do—well, practically anything!

HOW TO GET OUT OF DEBT—AND STAY OUT OF DEBT!

Are you in debt? Do your personal debts hold you back from getting the financing you need for business opportunities? If you answered YES, here's a solution for you.

Debtors Anonymous: A Proven Path to Financial Freedom

Debtors Anonymous is a self-help program designed to help people get out of debt—and stay out of debt. It works much like Weight Watchers, Gamblers Anonymous, and Alcoholics Anonymous, providing structure and support to help members take control of their finances and break free from debt.

If you or someone you know could benefit from this program, contact Debtors Anonymous Headquarters:

Debtors Anonymous General Service Office
PO Box 920888, Needham, MA 02492-0009
Phone: (781) 453-2743
Fax: (781) 453-2745

You can also check for local meetings in your area (please note that meeting locations and contact details may change).

Take Control—And Feel the Freedom!

Escaping personal debt gives you a powerful sense of freedom. However, business debt is a different story. When used wisely, business debt can be a tool for growth.

Here's why:

- **Business debts are often backed by collateral.** This provides security if repayment becomes difficult.
- **Businesses generate income.** That income can be used—fully or partially—to repay debts.
- **Business loans fund income-producing ventures.** Ideally, the money borrowed helps create profits that pay off the debt over time.

Debt: Use It Wisely, or It Will Use You!

Even though personal and business debt serve different purposes, both require careful management. The key is to stay in control and borrow strategically.

- Used wisely, debt can help you build wealth.
- Used recklessly, debt can drain your peace of mind—and your fortune.

The bottom line? Guard against unnecessary debt every day. Use it as a tool for financial growth—but handle it with extreme care!

GET LOANS EVEN WHEN YOUR CREDIT IS BAD, BAD, BAD!

Bad credit is a common plight of many people worldwide today. Many people abused their credit during their youth before they realized how important good credit is. Many people accepted credit cards before they knew how to control their spending urges; they then went on spending sprees, racking up big debts. Job loss, illness, marital problems, or other conditions led to unpaid credit card bills.

With so many people suffering from bad credit in the world today, lenders decided that this could be a good market for them—offering loans to such people. So today we see lender ads saying—among many other things:

- Bad Credit OK
- Consolidate Your Debt
- Easy Cash Solution

- Direct Banker!
- Quick & Easy First & Second Mortgages
- Borrow Up to 125% of the Value of Your Home

So how can you—or your client, if you're a consultant—benefit from lenders who specialize in what's called "D" credit? You can do several things you can't with conventional "perfect-credit-needed" lenders, namely:

- ❒ **Seek lenders who specialize in less-than-perfect-credit borrowers because with them poor credit is not a sin!**
- ❒ **Look over each lender's offers—see which lender's offer fits your—or your client's—situation best.**
- ❒ **Apply to the lender you've chosen, just by asking for their loan application and written loan requirements.**
- ❒ **Properly complete an online application or type a paper one.** Even with bad credit, a properly filled-out online form or a typed paper application looks better than a handwritten one!
- ❒ **Try to comply with all the lender's requirements.** Thus, if you must own real estate to qualify with a particular lender, don't apply unless you do own real estate. Seek a lender who makes "D" loans without the need for every borrower to own real estate.
- ❒ **Be willing to pay the interest rate the lender charges.** With "D" credit, you're really not in a position to argue over interest rates! Take what's offered to get your loan. Plan to refinance in a year or two if you think the rate you're being charged is too high. But get the loan!

High-risk "D" credit lenders are located almost all over. You can find these lenders in your area by looking in your local newspaper business and real estate pages, or by searching online lending directories.

USE PRIVATE LENDERS FOR HARD-TO-GET LOANS

Beginning wealth builders sometimes have trouble getting loans. Yet they often overlook one great source of loans—namely, private lenders.

And just what is a private lender? Here's your answer:

- An individual, or group of individuals, who make loans for business, real estate, and personal use to earn interest income from their excess funds.
- Lending on deals they like because the business appeals to them, they like the individual, or they think the business has great future earnings promise.
- Doing their lending for a second income, not their primary income. Lending is not their main source of income—a job or business is No. 1.
- Never seeking or accepting deposits from anyone, anywhere. A private lender is NOT a bank, NOT a credit union, and NOT a mortgage company. Instead, a private lender is usually an individual or group of individuals seeking good deals to lend on.
- Not required to follow local banking regulations—because they're not banks!

So what kinds of loans might you get from private lenders?

The two main types of loans made by private lenders are real estate and business loans. Personal loans are also made, but less frequently.

Real estate loans include:

- First mortgages, second mortgages, third mortgages, and beyond
- Down payment loans

- Property improvement loans
- "Wrap" loans
- Property "swap" loans
- And many other types

Business loans include:

- Business purchase loans
- Machinery purchase or repair
- Advertising expenses
- Employee training
- Building expansion or rehab
- Construction of new facilities

Personal loans include:

- Auto financing
- Real estate purchases
- Education expenses
- Medical and dental costs
- Debt consolidation
- Vacations
- Furniture purchases

How can you get a loan from a private lender?

Here are the easy steps to secure a private lender loan:

- ❒ **Locate a private lender who offers the type of loan you need.** See below for sources of private loans in various regions.
- ❒ **Contact "your" private lender and request details of their loan terms—called lending parameters.**
- ❒ **Fill out the required forms and submit your application.** If applying online, make sure all fields are

completed properly. If submitting on paper, type your loan application for a professional look.

- ❒ **Never pay upfront fees for any loan!** Legitimate private lenders do not require advance payments.

To find private lenders, look for them in:

- **ATTAIN: The IW$ Newsletter Money Available pages**
- **Your local large-city newspaper (Sunday edition)**
- **Magazines serving your industry**
- **Trade group publications**
- **Specialty financial journals**
- **Online lending directories and investment forums**

USE PERSONAL LOANS TO BUILD YOUR WEALTH

Personal loans can be powerful when you're seeking money for a business you want to start or expand. A personal loan:

- **Is a loan you get without putting up any collateral other than your signature on the application and loan agreement.**
- **Can run from 12 months to 60 months, with one monthly payment to the lender.**
- **Is available for a variety of purposes, such as vacation, education, medical, dental, moving, home improvement, taxes, tuition, miscellaneous expenses, and debt consolidation.**
- **Can be obtained in as little as 60 minutes ("The One-Hour Loan") from some lenders.** Other lenders give an answer—and a check—within 24 hours. Either way, you're not left waiting for weeks!
- **Is a powerful tool for new business owners who**

need cash for startup expenses, inventory, advertising, or unexpected costs.

- **Can be easier to get than a business loan for the same amount because no financial statements are required for a personal loan, while they are for a business loan.**
- **Is usually available in amounts from $1,000 to $50,000, depending on the lender, the borrower's credit rating, and annual income.**

To get a personal loan, you must have a good credit rating. Why? Because the "collateral" you offer is nothing more than ink on a piece of paper. So the only way a lender can protect the money loaned to you is:

- By ensuring you are a good credit risk. And a good credit risk means having a strong credit rating!
- By using your past credit history as a guide to how you will act with a new loan that must be repaid.

But what about a person with a poor credit rating? This is where most people have problems with personal loans. A poor credit rating means a person has:

- A history of "slow pays" on debts in the past.
- A recent bankruptcy.
- Judgments against them for failing to pay a debt.
- Other negative marks on their credit report.

How can a person get around such a record? There are several good, legitimate ways to secure a personal loan even with bad credit:

- ❒ **Get a cosigner with a good credit rating to sign your loan application.** This can be a friend, relative, spouse, or business associate.
- ❒ **Get a comaker with a good credit rating who is**

willing to be an equal partner on your loan. This person can be anyone listed above.

- ❒ **Get a guarantor—a person or organization that guarantees repayment of your loan if you are unable or unwilling to do so.** Again, your guarantor can be anyone from the list above.

8 SIGNATURE LOAN SECRETS FOR EVERYONE

Signature loans, also called personal loans, consumer loans, unsecured loans, and "anything" loans by some lenders, have several distinct features that set them apart from other loans, namely:

- **The only collateral is a bit of ink on a piece of paper.** The lender does not have any hard assets (real estate, stocks, bonds, or savings accounts) to claim if the borrower fails to repay.
- **Most signature loans have terms of three years or less.** The shorter the loan term, the lower the risk for the lender.
- **Few companies qualify for signature loans.** Most businesses have equipment or real estate to pledge as collateral. A signature loan is, by definition, a personal loan—not a business loan.

Knowing these facts about signature loans can make it easier for you to get one. Here are your eight secrets to getting your personal loan faster, easier, and with fewer questions or problems:

1. Apply only to a signature loan lender for a signature loan! Obvious, you say? Not so—plenty of people apply to real estate lenders for a signature loan. It does not work.
2. Don't ask for too large a loan. Most signature loan

lenders cap loans at $35,000, and most prefer amounts between $1,500 and $15,000.

3. If your credit is weak, strengthen it upfront by bringing in a cosigner with good credit. This helps you avoid a rejection, which stays on your credit file for nine months.
4. Properly complete an online application or type a paper one. While it's not a business loan, a neatly filled-out application gets faster and better attention than the hundreds of sloppy ones a lender sees every year!
5. Use the lender's official loan application. Don't try to submit a form from another lender. It will only get you a quick NO.
6. Apply for an approved purpose only. Signature loans are commonly used for debt consolidation, vacations, education, and miscellaneous expenses. If you try to force a lender to approve a loan for something outside their criteria, you won't get the loan.
7. Seek local lenders first. You and they talk the same language, may have shared connections or local references, and can establish trust more easily than with a lender across the country.
8. Be pleasant and cooperative with the lender. Never forget: Honey gets more YES answers than vinegar!

Know your lender, follow these eight tips, and get your signature loan now! A signature loan can put you in business!

GETTING THE LOAN YOU NEED WHEN SOME LENDERS SAY NO

Some people seeking loans have less-than-perfect credit. So they get a lot of NO answers when they apply for a loan. What can be done to turn a NO into a YES?

Here are a number of useful ways to get your loan despite refusals:

- ❐ **Apply to different lenders.** If you've been applying at banks for a real estate loan, try mortgage lenders listed in online business directories or financial websites.
- ❐ **Reduce or increase the amount you're trying to borrow.** Some lenders will gladly lend you less than you're applying for. Others will lend only larger amounts—say $500,000 or more per loan.
- ❐ **Find out why you've been turned down—then adjust.** If your credit is weak, get a cosigner. If you're told "too many inquiries on your credit report," seek out lenders who don't place too much weight on that factor.
- ❐ **Strengthen your credit BEFORE you apply.** Do this by getting a cosigner, comaker, or guarantor for your loan.
- ❐ **Go to the right type of lender.** A real estate lender for a real estate loan, a business lender for a business loan, etc.
- ❐ **Apply to lots of lenders.** Don't stop after a few rejections! One borrower we know of applied at 462 lenders for a $700,000 real estate mortgage. All 462 lenders said NO—but lender No. 463 said YES!
- ❐ **Ask each lender why you were turned down.** Take steps to correct the issue. Over time, your application will become fine-tuned to a YES answer!
- ❐ **Talk to lenders—either by phone, video call, or in person.** Learn what types of loans they prefer, loan terms, interest rates, and approval criteria.
- ❐ **Listen to what the lender says!** You're not learning

while you're talking! A few minutes with a lender can provide a college education in the art of borrowing money for yourself or your business.

- ❒ **"Position" your loan so it's within the lender's preferred range.** If a lender typically funds $100,000 loans, apply for that amount.
- ❒ **Use ONLY the lender's loan application.** Do not submit forms from another lender—you'll be rejected instantly.
- ❒ **Properly complete an online loan application or type a paper one.** Attractive, professional-looking applications get reviewed faster and receive more YES answers than sloppy, scribbled ones.

Thousands of loan applicants get the loan they seek—because they keep looking!

USING ENTHUSIASM TO GET BUSINESS LOANS OF ALL KINDS

If you don't have credit or collateral, can you still get business or real estate loans?

Yes, you can! How? By using the power of persuasion, like this:

- ❒ **Prepare a plan for the business, showing what you will do after you take it over and what its sales will be in the first, second, and third year.**
- ❒ **List, in your plan, the steps you will take to improve the business or real estate.** Show the expected results in higher sales, better rental income, and larger profits.
- ❒ **Show your plan to the seller.** Explain how much stronger and more profitable the business will be under your management, using the strategies outlined

in your plan—which need not be more than two or three typed pages.

❒ **Get the seller to finance your down payment.** How? Use any of these proven methods:

- **Take back a mortgage.** This is called a purchase-money (PM) mortgage. Your plan will show how the income from the business will pay off this loan. The rest of the seller's payment comes from a long-term mortgage on the business or real estate.
- **Have the seller take out an equity loan.** You assume this loan and make all payments on it. Your plan should show how you will afford these payments based on business income.
- **Use a personal line of credit or personal loan for the down payment.** Apply online or through your bank or credit union. Repay it on time, using the income from the business.
- **Leverage the assets of the business or real estate as collateral.** Many businesses are bought using their own assets! This is called a leveraged buyout (LBO)—where you use the land, machines, and buildings the business owns as collateral for the loan to acquire it.

❒ **Show great enthusiasm for the business, its future potential, and its importance to employees and the community.** Enthusiasm is a powerful convincer and can make a seller choose you over other buyers.

❒ **Have an attorney advise you.** Never enter into a business or real estate purchase without legal guidance. A competent attorney will protect you from pitfalls and help you get a better deal.

Enthusiasm can overcome all kinds of objections. Liking a business you want to buy is a key secret to success. Start using this key NOW!

EASIER WAYS TO GET LOANS FROM PRIVATE LENDERS

Do you have weak or "bad" credit? A recent bankruptcy? Do you know people in these situations? If you do, then we have an answer for you that's worth considering. And that answer is:

- If you're trying to get a personal, business, or real estate loan, consider using a private lender instead of a bank or small finance company because:
- Private lenders are often willing to take greater risks since they are looking for higher interest earnings on the money they lend.
- You can negotiate more easily with a private lender because most are individuals who can be spoken to directly without rigid rules or bureaucracy.

So if a private lender interests you, follow these easy steps to get your loan quickly and at the lowest cost:

❒ **Decide what type of loan you need—personal, business, or real estate.** You must know this before you apply.

❒ **Write out, in simple language, the reasons for your bad credit.** Perhaps you had a job loss, illness, divorce, or family emergency.

❒ **Demonstrate that you are reliable and honest.** Make it clear that outside circumstances—not carelessness—caused your credit problems.

❒ **Ask for a specific loan amount—$10,000,**

$25,000, $75,000, etc. Never ask the lender to decide for you! Know exactly how much you need.

- ❒ **Describe the purpose of your loan.** Whether it's to start a business, buy real estate, pay off debts, or consolidate existing loans, be specific.
- ❒ **Explain how you plan to repay the loan.** A clear repayment plan impresses private lenders and shows you appreciate the trust they're extending to you.
- ❒ **Offer any collateral you may have—such as your home, car, boat, or jewelry.** This demonstrates your sincerity.
- ❒ **Send your loan request electronically.** Private lenders accept applications via email, online forms, or secure document uploads. Typed and professionally formatted applications always make a better impression than handwritten ones.

Where can you find private lenders?

Most private lenders can be found through online lending platforms, business funding networks, and private investment groups. Look in:

- Online private lending directories
- Business and real estate financing marketplaces
- Investor forums and peer-to-peer lending websites
- Professional networking platforms for investors and lenders

Many lenders advertise on these trusted online platforms, making it easier than ever to connect with private lenders nationwide.

If you're struggling to get a loan through traditional lenders, a private lender may provide the solution you need.

THE CREDIT CARD DEAL THAT'S HARD TO BEAT

More people than ever use credit cards to start and grow a business. And banks keep seeking more card customers. Many banks offer cards with low interest rates, credit lines of $50,000 and up, cashback rebates, and other perks.

Here's what every Beginning Wealth Builder (BWB) should know about using credit-card credit to fund a new business:

- **Credit cards—used wisely—have countless good uses for BWBs.** Look for offbeat ways to use them (see below).
- **Focus on using your cards for long-term benefits—and only for things you truly need.**
- **Keep credit-card credit handy for critical times.**
- **Get short-term financing—"interest-free."** A smart manufacturing business owner charges $30,000 in supplies on two cards each month. Thirty days later, he pays the bill in full. "It's like a 30-day, $30,000 loan with no interest charge," he says.
- **Get good interest rates without a lot of paperwork.** A BWB wine exporter spent months securing a $50,000 government loan. Later, she and her partner signed up for 16 low-interest-rate credit cards. Using the cards, they got over $40,000 in cash advances overnight. Their average interest rate was 12.5%—just 1% higher than the government loan's rate.

Of course, credit cards aren't for everyone. People who pay late or buy things their business doesn't need should look for other money sources.

Also, some credit cards work well for some people but not for others. If a bank offers you a corporate credit card, be careful. Corporate cards often have higher fees and additional costs.

Follow these easy steps to use credit-card credit to help finance your new business:

- ❒ **Select only cards that your merchants and suppliers accept.**
- ❒ **Apply for multiple cards if you think you'll need a large cash reserve.**
- ❒ **Sign up for cards before quitting your regular job.**
- ❒ **Avoid:**
    - Application fees
    - "900" number application lines
    - High APRs and high annual fees
    - Cards with unnecessary frills (Online tools like CardTrak provide up-to-date lists of the lowest interest rates and fees.)
- ❒ **Combine credit-card money with a conventional bank loan for greater funding power.**
- ❒ **Get interest-free credit.** How? Pay credit card bills in full each month, if possible.
- ❒ **Check your credit-card interest rates and budget monthly to avoid surprises if rates change.**
- ❒ **Call the bank(s) that issued your credit cards:**
    - When a card's low introductory rate expires, ask for a smaller increase. Banks may agree to raise it by 5% instead of 8%—or whatever you can negotiate.
    - Two to three weeks before your annual fee is billed, call your credit card issuer. Tell them you want to remain a customer and ask them to waive the annual fee.
- ❒ **Transfer balances from high-interest cards to low-**

er-interest ones. But first, confirm that your bank won't charge a hefty transfer fee!

- ❐ **Keep business charges separate from personal ones.** This makes bookkeeping easier.
- ❐ **Avoid late payments like the plague.** Late payments will only hurt you in the long run.

THE AFFINITY CARD WAY TO CREDIT-CARD WEALTH

Getting loans is much easier when you have an established line of credit with a bank or other lender. And the easiest way to get such a line of credit (which is really, in effect, a preapproved loan) is to have as many credit cards as possible. For example:

- Some people have as many as 20 credit cards in their own name.
- Each card has a credit limit ranging from $500 to $25,000, depending on how much the person requested when opening the card.
- Many cards come with check-writing privileges or cash advance options, allowing you to start your credit line by simply writing a check or making a transfer for what you need, up to your limit.

What most people don't know is there's an easier way to get multiple credit cards today. This method is also great for getting your first credit card. What's the method?

- Look for, and apply for, an "affinity card."
- Affinity cards are special credit cards issued in partnership with nonprofit groups or social causes that the cardholder supports—such as the National Wildlife Federation or the Winter Olympics.
- Your affinity card features the logo of the group you're supporting. For example, if you get a football affinity

card, you might choose the team you like, and its logo and colors will appear on your card.

- Getting an affinity card is easier than a standard credit card. Why? Because issuers are eager to sign up new customers who will generate interest income while also supporting a cause.

To get an affinity card for yourself, take these easy steps.

- ❒ **Find out which banks or financial institutions offer affinity cards.** Check online banking websites, financial service platforms, and affinity card directories. Many affinity cards are advertised on bank websites and credit comparison tools.
- ❒ **Apply for affinity cards that match your interests.** Watch for digital ads, direct mail offers, or email promotions. Apply to every card that appeals to you.
- ❒ **Fill out an application for each affinity card.** Key idea: You're supporting a good cause while using an affinity card. (It does not cost you anything extra—the card issuer donates a portion of its proceeds.)
- ❒ **If asked why you're applying for multiple cards, be honest.** Explain that you want to support the affiliated cause.
- ❒ **Request the largest credit limit possible.** Don't be bashful—if you don't ask for a higher limit, you won't get it!

Keep applying for affinity cards until you have as many as you need. That way, you'll have far more loan credit than you ever thought possible!

10 FAST WAYS TO TURN BAD CREDIT INTO GOOD CREDIT

Many people with bad credit feel "locked in." They feel like they can't get a loan, can't buy a car on credit, and can't qualify for a mortgage to buy a home.

Result? They feel stuck—with nowhere to turn for help.

Here's help in these easy steps that almost anyone can take, starting today:

1. **Get a cosigner for any loan you apply for.**
   Have the cosigner ready BEFORE you apply for the loan. Don't wait until you're turned down—being prepared in advance increases your chances of getting a YES.

2. **Buy a home or car with joint ownership.**
   Partner with someone who has good credit—this offsets the bad credit of one applicant. Every salesperson wants to close a sale—they'll focus on the good-credit applicant.

3. **Apply to lenders who handle less-than-perfect credit applications.**
   These are often called "hard-money" lenders or "C and D" credit lenders. They specialize in higher-risk loans and may approve your application when traditional banks won't.

4. **Use reputable credit-repair agencies to apply for loans on your behalf.**
   Many nonprofit credit-repair agencies present credit-rebuilding plans along with loan applications to lenders who are willing to work with borrowers who are sincerely trying to improve their credit.

5. **Form a company—sole proprietorship, partner-**

ship, or corporation—and have your business apply for the loan.
Many lenders routinely approve business loans more easily than personal loans.

6. **Get one or more credit cards with a suitable credit line—$5,000, $10,000, etc.**
Secure these credit cards with a cosigner, the help of a credit-repair agency, or through your business. Some business credit cards offer up to $100,000 in credit to their business account holders.

7. **Apply for a grant instead of a loan.**
Grantmakers seldom check credit. Instead, they are interested in the importance of the work you'll do and your ability to do it well.

8. **Have collateral ready before applying for a loan.**
When you offer collateral upfront, lenders focus on the security of the loan instead of your credit score.

9. **Explore city, state, or federal government loan sources.**
Many government-backed loan programs have "helping" clauses in their charters. These programs are designed to lend to people recovering from personal financial hardships or past business losses.

10. **Keep applying for the loan you need.**
Never take NO for an answer! Every time you apply, you learn how to present a stronger application.

Sooner or later, your answer will be YES—making you forget all the NOs!

GOOD PLANNING—EASIER LOANS

Nearly anyone can increase their chances of getting a loan. First, they need to do a little planning. Here are some basic points and specific suggestions to show how good planning can help you secure a loan more easily.

Draw up a simple plan. Answer the following questions as best as you can. You can do this yourself or get help from a consultant, accountant, or a knowledgeable friend.

- ❒ **How much do you need to borrow?**
  Try to find a sensible range—both high and low amounts—that can meet your needs. Lenders prefer borrowers who are flexible. Being demanding and stubborn will not impress them.
- ❒ **Where will you focus your loan search?**
  Should you look for lenders locally, regionally, or nationally? Keep in mind that many lenders only offer smaller loans (under $100,000) in their local areas. If you're seeking a small loan, start with local banks or commercial finance companies.
- ❒ **Which lenders might be a good match for you?**
  Find out what types of businesses and loans each lender specializes in. You can research this online or by calling lenders directly. You don't have to give your name to ask general questions.
  Example: If you're in the business of buying historic buildings, don't waste time on a lender that only funds international medical firms.
- ❒ **How will you use the money?** Will you rent a 10,000-square-foot office? Buy a fire truck and 60 nozzles? Pay four employees for a year?
- ❒ **Be specific.** Lenders want to see that you have a well-thought-out plan for using their money.
- ❒ **How will you secure the loan and pay it off?**
  What collateral can you offer? Are you proposing any special repayment methods—such as making advance payments?

- ❐ **Be ready to explain:**
  - How much you can afford to pay per month
  - How long you need to repay the loan

To finish your simple plan, take the following steps:

- ❐ **Contact prospective lenders.**
  - Request their loan application materials and ask about their borrowing requirements. Most banks require:
    1. A business plan
    2. A balance sheet
    3. An income statement (or for new companies, an estimated future income report).
- ❐ **Ask for outside help if needed.** If you're unsure about the paperwork or any part of the process, get assistance.
- ❐ **You don't have to hire an accountant to get a loan—but it can help.** Some lenders see an accountant's work as a sign of a well-prepared loan application.
- ❐ **Other sources of help include:**
  - Other business owners
  - Friends or family members with financial knowledge
  - Organizations like IW$ that specialize in loan preparation
- ❐ **Take a break and sleep on it.** Step away from the loan process for a short time. When you return, what once seemed complicated may now feel much easier.

The big thing about planning is that good planning organizes your thoughts and actions around your goal of getting a loan. This removes much of the guesswork and helps you make a strong impression on lenders.

HOW TO GET A LOAN WITHOUT THE BEST OF CREDIT

Many people need a loan for business or personal use, but their credit isn't in the best shape. What can be done to improve credit to the point where a needed loan can be obtained?

Here are some effective strategies:

- ❒ **Get a cosigner who accepts responsibility for the loan if the borrower does not repay.** The cosigner must have a stronger credit rating than the borrower, so the lender is more willing to approve the loan.
- ❒ **Pledge collateral that the lender can claim if the loan is not repaid.** This collateral can be pledged by either the borrower or a cosigner.
- ❒ **Borrow with a comaker.** A comaker is different from a cosigner. A comaker is an equal borrower, while a cosigner only steps in if the loan is not repaid.
- ❒ **Get a surety bond to guarantee repayment of the loan.** Surety bonds are issued by surety companies, which can be found through online insurance and bonding directories. A surety bond typically costs 2% to 5% of the loan amount.
- ❒ **Put the loan under a business name instead of your personal name.** If your business has stronger credit than you do, applying under the company name may increase approval chances.
- ❒ **Use home equity as collateral.** A home equity loan (on your home or a relative's home) can provide funding for any purpose. Home equity loans now allow borrowing up to 125% of home value. Example: If your home is worth $100,000, and you owe $80,000 on it, your equity is $20,000. But at 125% financing: 1.25 x $100,000 = $125,000; $125,000

- $80,000 = $45,000 available. This means you can borrow far more than your existing equity in hopes that the property value increases over time.

- ❐ **Rent collateral to pledge for the loan.** Some wealthy investors offer collateral for rent in exchange for a one-time fee of 5% to 10% of the loan amount. Example: Renting $100,000 in collateral would typically cost $5,000 to $10,000.

Using any of these, or a combination of these, methods could get you the loan you need!

> ***What you must always keep in mind is that lenders WANT to lend—but they also want to reduce their risk.***

The methods above give lenders the assurance that the loan WILL be repaid, even if the borrower defaults!

GET CREDIT WHERE PEOPLE LOVE TO GIVE IT

Credit cards will give you "instant" credit—usually in about two minutes. We call this almost instant. Take this example:

A cardholder charged $53 million on a credit card to buy three airplanes. The charge was approved in 2.5 minutes (about 30 seconds longer than usual). The cardholder then flew off in one of the planes—purchased entirely on a credit card.

Nearly $10 million per minute—24 hours a day—is charged to credit cards. Why not tap into this money flow for your business or real estate use?

> ***The best places to get credit are where people love to give it. To secure this kind of credit, you will need an "average" or "good" credit record.***

What does that mean? A credit history without recent nonpayments or late payments. If you need help improving your credit, see the articles elsewhere in this section.

Now:

1. **Get as many credit cards as you can—the more, the better!**
2. **Request the largest credit line possible on each card.**
   A credit line costs you nothing until you use it!
3. **Pay bills on time—improve your credit while increasing your wealth.**
4. **Keep searching for new cards daily—the more, the better!**

Open more doors with an instant line of credit

A line of credit is different from a credit card. A line of credit is a loan you use gradually, instead of all at once. With a $100,000 line of credit, a lender gives you the ability to:

- Write checks for up to $100,000 for business or personal use.
- Withdraw funds with the understanding that you will start repayments at a scheduled time.
- You can get an instant line of credit from most lenders that have issued you a credit card.

Some credit card issuers offer lines of credit up to $40,000 per card, with some considering $50,000 limits.

Example of a credit card-based line of credit:

Card No. 1: Line of credit = $7,500

Card No. 2: Line of credit = $10,000

Card No. 3: Line of credit = $35,000

Total line of credit = $52,500

To build a bigger line of credit...

- ❒ **Get more credit cards!**
- ❒ **If a local card issuer denies you with the excuse "You have enough cards already," simply thank them and move on.**
- ❒ **Apply to multiple lenders—both locally and nationally.**
- ❒ **Expand your search:**
- ❒ **Apply online or through financial comparison platforms for national card issuers.**
- ❒ **Keep applications going out regularly.**

HOW TO USE CREDIT CARDS FOR SUCCESS

The easiest kind of credit to get today is credit on a major credit card, because:

- Credit card issuers want more cards in circulation so they can earn interest on card usage.
- Credit cards are easy for issuers to control—users can't extend their own credit beyond set limits, and issuers can stop credit if needed.
- Credit card earnings are highly profitable for issuers, creating a natural incentive to approve more accounts.

Remember these key facts about credit card money:

- **The dollar you get from a credit card loan is as good as a dollar from any other loan.**
- **Credit card requirements are often simpler and easier to meet than loan requirements.**
- **You can hold multiple credit cards—but it is generally harder to get multiple loans.**
- **You can use credit card money for any legal purpose.** Most loan applications restrict how you use the money. Example: A business loan requires you to spend the money on the specific business purpose

listed on your application. A credit card, however, allows you to buy goods or services for home or business—without restrictions.

To get multiple credit cards, each with its own separate line of credit...

- ❒ **Apply online for the fastest results.** Visit the bank's website, credit card issuers' platforms, or financial comparison websites to find and apply for cards instantly. Many banks offer instant pre-approvals online.
- ❒ **Fill out online applications carefully.** Ensure all information is accurate and complete. Online applications are processed quickly, and errors can cause delays or denials.
- ❒ **If applying for multiple cards, submit all applications on the same day.** This allows all applications to process simultaneously. Many banks and issuers conduct soft credit checks first, so you can gauge approval chances without hurting your credit score.
- ❒ **Once you get a card—USE IT!** Make a purchase, then pay off the balance as soon as the bill arrives. Show issuers that you're a responsible borrower!
- ❒ **If an issuer denies your application, wait six months and reapply.** Most issuers clear rejected applications every six months, so you'll be treated as a new applicant. Meanwhile, apply to other issuers as well.

Is it really worth getting lots of cards?

Sometimes, but not always. If you want a line of credit, having multiple cards might be useful. Of course, credit card money must be repaid. If you use credit for business or real estate, your positive cash flow will generate the funds you need to pay off your balance.

Every on-time payment improves your credit rating.

More available credit and an improving credit score? That's a win-win!

APPENDIX I

CREDIT LAW & CONSUMER PROTECTIONS

Understanding your rights as a borrower is essential to protecting your credit, avoiding scams, and ensuring fair treatment from lenders. The following federal laws govern how credit is reported, billed, and issued.

FAIR CREDIT REPORTING ACT (FCRA)

What It Does

- Ensures that credit reporting agencies (Experian, Equifax, TransUnion) provide accurate, fair, and private credit information.
- Gives consumers the right to access and dispute errors on their credit reports.

Your Rights Under the FCRA

- You can get a free credit report from each bureau once a year at AnnualCreditReport.com.
- If information is inaccurate, you can dispute it, and the credit bureau must investigate within 30 days.
- Only authorized parties (lenders, employers, landlords) can access your credit report.

How to Take Action

- ❒ **Request your free report and check for errors.**
- ❒ **Dispute any inaccuracies online or by mail with the credit bureau.**
- ❒ **Set up a credit freeze or fraud alert if you suspect identity theft.**

FAIR CREDIT BILLING ACT (FCBA)

What It Does

- Protects consumers from billing errors, unauthorized charges, and unfair credit practices on credit card statements.
- Establishes a dispute process for incorrect charges.

Your Rights Under the FCBA

- You have 60 days from the billing date to dispute errors.
- The credit card issuer must acknowledge the dispute within 30 days and resolve it within two billing cycles (90 days max).
- You do not have to pay the disputed amount while it's under investigation.

How to Take Action

❒ **Check your statements every month for errors or unauthorized charges.**

❒ **If you find an error, send a written dispute to your card issuer's billing inquiries department.**

❒ **Keep records of all communication related to your dispute.**

EQUAL CREDIT OPPORTUNITY ACT (ECOA)

What It Does

Ensures fair access to credit by prohibiting discrimination based on:

- Race or national origin
- Gender, age, or marital status
- Religion
- Income source (e.g., Social Security, disability benefits, public assistance)

Your Rights Under the ECOA

- Lenders must consider only your creditworthiness—not personal factors.
- You have the right to receive a written explanation if denied credit.
- Married couples can apply for credit separately without requiring a spouse's signature (except in certain cases, such as shared property states).

How to Take Action

❒ **If denied credit, request a reason in writing within 30 days.**

❒ **If you believe discrimination played a role, file a complaint with the Consumer Financial Protection Bureau (CFPB) at consumerfinance.gov.**

APPENDIX II

FEDERAL AGENCIES AND ASSISTANCE

If you need assistance with credit-related issues, disputes, or consumer protections, the following agencies provide valuable resources and support. Instead of relying on printed contact information, which may change over time, visit their official websites for the most up-to-date information and guidance.

Each agency provides an online complaint system and additional contact options. If you're facing a credit dispute, fraud, or need loan assistance, start by visiting their website and following their official complaint procedures.

- ❒ **Consumer Financial Protection Bureau** (CFPB)
  For complaints about banks, credit cards, loans, and financial services, visit: *www.consumerfinance.gov*
- ❒ **Federal Trade Commission** (FTC)
  For credit reporting, identity theft, and unfair lending practices, visit: *www.ftc.gov*
- ❒ **Federal Reserve System**
  For information on banking regulations and consumer protections, visit: *www.federalreserve.gov*
- ❒ **Office of the Comptroller of the Currency** (OCC)
  For issues related to national banks and federal savings associations, visit: *www.occ.gov*
- ❒ **Federal Deposit Insurance Corporation** (FDIC)
  For information on insured banks, deposit protection, and consumer rights, visit: *www.fdic.gov*

- ❒ **National Credit Union Administration (NCUA)**
  For assistance with federally insured credit unions, visit: *www.ncua.gov*
- ❒ **U.S. Small Business Administration (SBA)**
  For business credit, loan programs, and financial assistance: *www.sba.gov*
- ❒ **U.S. Department of Housing and Urban Development (HUD)**
  For mortgage assistance, housing discrimination, and FHA loan issues: *www.hud.gov*
- ❒ **Internal Revenue Service (IRS): Taxpayer Advocate Service**
  For tax-related identity theft, IRS liens affecting credit, and financial relief programs: *www.irs.gov/advocate*
- ❒ **Department of Justice (DOJ): Consumer Protection Branch**
  For enforcement of consumer protection laws against fraud, predatory lending, and scams: *www.justice.gov/civil/consumer-protection-branch*
- ❒ **Better Business Bureau (BBB) (Not a government agency but useful for disputes)**
  For checking lender reputations, filing complaints, and avoiding scams: *www.bbb.org*

GLOSSARY

Annual Percentage Rate (APR). The cost of credit expressed as a yearly percentage, including interest and fees.

Appraisal Fee. A charge for determining the market value of property used as loan collateral.

Asset. Property or financial resources that can be used to repay debt, such as real estate, stocks, or vehicles.

Automated Teller Machines (ATMs). Electronic kiosks that allow users to withdraw cash, check balances, and transfer funds.

Balloon Payment. A large final payment due at the end of a loan or lease term, often used in real estate and auto financing.

Billing Error. A mistake in a credit card or loan statement, as defined by the Fair Credit Billing Act.

Business Days. The days a financial institution operates for business transactions, which may vary by bank.

Charge-off. When a creditor writes off an unpaid debt as a loss, typically after 180 days of non-payment, though the borrower still owes the debt.

Collateral. Property pledged as security for a loan, which can be seized if the borrower defaults.

Cosigner. A person who agrees to take legal responsibility for repaying a loan if the primary borrower fails to do so.

Credit. The ability to borrow money or receive goods and services with an agreement to repay later.

Credit Bureau. An agency that collects and maintains consumer credit information, such as Experian, Equifax, and TransUnion.

Credit Card. A payment card that allows users to borrow money up to a set limit, requiring at least minimum monthly payments.

Credit History. A record of a borrower's past use of credit, including payment history, debt levels, and account longevity.

Credit Inquiry. A request to check a person's credit report. Soft inquiries do not affect credit scores, while hard inquiries may impact them.

Credit Limit. The maximum amount a borrower can charge on a credit card or revolving credit account.

Credit Report. A detailed history of an individual's borrowing and repayment behavior, used by lenders to assess creditworthiness.

Credit Score. A numerical rating, typically between 300-850, that represents a borrower's creditworthiness based on their credit history.

Credit Scoring System. A statistical model used by lenders to evaluate a borrower's creditworthiness.

Credit Utilization Ratio. The percentage of available credit a person is using; lower ratios generally indicate better credit health.

Creditworthiness. An assessment of a borrower's ability to repay debts based on financial history and current obligations.

Debt-to-Income Ratio (DTI). A percentage that compares a borrower's total monthly debt payments to their gross monthly income, used to assess loan eligibility.

Debit Card (EFT Card). A payment card that deducts funds directly from a checking account, unlike a credit card.

Default. Failure to meet the legal obligation of a loan, such as missing payments.

Deferment. A temporary pause on loan payments, often used for student loans, during which interest may or may not accrue.

Disclosures. Required information lenders must provide about loan terms, interest rates, and fees.

Elderly Applicant. A person aged 62 or older, as defined under the Equal Credit Opportunity Act.

Electronic Fund Transfer (EFT). Any financial transaction made electronically, such as direct deposits, online payments, and ATM withdrawals.

Equity. The portion of an asset (such as a home) that the owner truly owns, calculated as the market value minus any outstanding loans.

Fair Credit Reporting Act (FCRA). A federal law that regulates how credit bureaus collect, share, and handle consumer credit information.

Finance Charge. The total cost of borrowing money, including interest and fees.

Fixed Interest Rate. An interest rate that remains unchanged for the life of a loan.

Forbearance. A temporary reduction or suspension of loan payments, typically granted due to financial hardship.

Hard Inquiry. A lender's request to check an applicant's credit report as part of a loan application, which may slightly lower credit scores.

Home Equity Line of Credit (HELOC). A revolving credit line that allows homeowners to borrow against the equity in their property.

Joint Account. A credit or bank account shared by two or more people, who are all legally responsible for the account's obligations.

Late Payment. A payment made after the due date, which may result in fees and negatively affect credit scores.

Lessee. A person who leases or rents property.

Lessor. A company or person that owns and leases property to another party.

Liability on an Account. The legal obligation to repay a debt.

Minimum Payment. The smallest amount a borrower must pay on a credit account each month to avoid penalties.

Mortgage. A loan used to finance the purchase of real estate, typically repaid in monthly installments over several years.

Open-End Credit. A revolving credit account that can be used repeatedly up to a set limit, such as a credit card or HELOC.

Overdraft Fee. A charge imposed when a checking account balance goes below zero due to a transaction exceeding available funds.

Point-of-Sale (POS) Transaction. A payment made electronically at a retail location using a debit or credit card.

Points (Mortgage Points). Prepaid interest fees paid at loan closing to reduce the interest rate over the loan's term.

Punitive Damages. Court-awarded damages intended to punish a creditor for violating credit laws.

Revolving Credit. A type of credit that allows borrowers to repeatedly access funds up to a set limit, as long as payments are made.

Rescission. The cancellation of a loan or credit agreement within a specified period, often used in home refinancing.

Secured Credit Card. A credit card backed by a cash deposit, often used to help build or rebuild credit.

Secured Loan. A loan backed by collateral, such as a car or house, which the lender can seize if the borrower defaults.

Security Interest. A lender's legal right to claim collateral if a borrower defaults on a loan.

Service Charge. A fee charged by a financial institution for account maintenance or transactions.

Soft Inquiry. A credit check that does not affect a person's credit score, such as when checking their own credit or during prequalification.

Subprime Loan. A loan offered to borrowers with poor credit, usually at higher interest rates due to increased risk.

Term Loan. A loan with a fixed repayment schedule and a specific end date.

Truth in Lending Act (TILA). A federal law requiring lenders to disclose loan terms, interest rates, and fees in a clear and understandable manner.

Unsecured Loan. A loan that does not require collateral, such as personal loans and most credit cards.

Wage Garnishment. A legal process where a portion of a debtor's wages is withheld by an employer to repay outstanding debts.

INDEX

TYLER G. HICKS

Tyler G. Hicks (June 21, 1921 – March 12, 2020) was a celebrated business author, financial innovator, and mentor who empowered countless individuals to achieve financial independence. Hicks spent nearly a century mastering and teaching the principles of wealth creation and entrepreneurship.

Over his prolific career, Hicks authored more than 100 books, including iconic titles such as *How to Acquire $1 Million in Income Real Estate in One Year Using Borrowed Money* (IWS-94) and *Smart Money Shortcuts to Becoming Rich* (IWS-71). His writings were known for their practical, no-nonsense advice, offering readers actionable steps to build businesses and invest wisely.

Hicks was the founder of International Wealth Success (IW$), a groundbreaking resource library dedicated to helping entrepreneurs and investors achieve their dreams. Through IW$, he pioneered innovative strategies for acquiring businesses, investing in real estate, and using "other people's money" (a term he coined) to grow wealth.

A trailblazer in his field, Tyler G. Hicks' legacy continues to inspire entrepreneurs around the world, proving that success is within reach for anyone willing to take bold and decisive action.

LEARN MORE AT ***iWealthSuccess.com.***

INTERNATIONAL WEALTH SUCCESS (IW$)

International Wealth Success (IW$) is your go-to resource for entrepreneurial success and financial freedom. IW$ began in 1966 with founder Tyler G. Hicks and remains the leading authority on business ownership, real estate investing, and proven financial strategies. IW$ provides powerful tools, expert guidance, and practical inspiration to help you build lasting wealth. IW$ is a proud member of Kallisti Publishing Inc., publishers of the books you need to succeed. If you can dream it, you can do it—and IW$ will show you how to move forward boldly!

- **Providing Actionable Knowledge.**
- **Cultivating Entrepreneurial Confidence.**
- **Supporting Diverse Wealth-Building Stages.**
- **Expanding Financial Literacy.**
- **Promoting Self-Reliance.**
- **Empowering Personal Growth.**
- **Inspiring Legacy Building.**
- **Providing a Proven Pathway to Success.**

IW$ empowers you to unlock your full wealth-building potential and embrace a future filled with prosperity and possibility. **Move forward boldly** at *iWealthSuccess.com*.

ATTAIN : *THE OFFICIAL IW$ COMPANION AND GUIDE TO WEALTH BUILDING*

ATTAIN is your ultimate resource for achieving financial independence and long-term success. Delivered 12 times a year, each issue is packed with actionable insights, proven strategies, and exclusive opportunities tailored to entrepreneurs and investors at all levels. Here's what you can expect:

- **Expert Wealth-Building Strategies** to maximize your success and accelerate growth.
- **Insider Tips and Techniques** for scaling your business and expanding your investments.
- **Real-World Examples and Proven Ideas** you can implement right away to drive results.
- **Updates on the Latest Tools, Resources, and Success Stories** from the IW$ community.

Move Forward Boldly! Subscribe to *ATTAIN* and unlock the strategies, tools, and connections to transform your financial future!

SUBSCRIBE NOW AT ***iWealthSuccess.com*** ...

IW$ BOOKS, KITS, AND ATTAIN

Since 1966, *International Wealth Success* has assembled a dynamic library of in-depth books and kits, as well as the world-renown *ATTAIN*, to help you build wealth as quickly and easily as possible. As a part of the Kallisti Publishing Inc. family, IW$ remains committed to preserving and expanding upon the legacy of the founder, Tyler G. Hicks, by offering products that inspire, educate, and equip individuals with the confidence to unlock their full financial potential.

BOOKS

IW$ features a curated collection of the best books on wealth-building, entrepreneurship, and financial success. With titles by Tyler G. Hicks and other industry experts, these books offer practical insights, proven strategies, and the knowledge you need to excel in business and investing.

SUCCESS KITS

IW$ Success Kits are self-study courses that guide you through selected types of independent businesses and real estate money making methods.

ATTAIN: THE OFFICIAL INTERNATIONAL WEALTH SUCCESS COMPANION AND GUIDE TO WEALTH BUILDING

ATTAIN is your ultimate resource for achieving financial independence and long-term success. Each issue is packed with actionable insights, proven strategies, and exclusive opportunities tailored to entrepreneurs and investors at all levels. Move Forward Boldly! Subscribe to *ATTAIN* and unlock the strategies, tools, and connections to transform your financial future!

VISIT THE IW$ WEBSITE AT *iWealthSuccess.com.*

If you can dream it,

then you can do it —

and IW$ will show you how!

www.IWEALTHSUCCESS.com

Made in the USA
Monee, IL
04 November 2026

67383624R00105